About Dogs

About Dogs

The 1977 Childcraft Annual

An annual supplement to
Childcraft–The How and Why Library

Field Enterprises Educational Corporation
Chicago Frankfurt London Paris Rome Sydney Tokyo Toronto
A subsidiary of
Field Enterprises, Inc.

Acknowledgments

The publishers of *Childcraft—The How and Why Library* gratefully acknowledge the courtesy of the following publishers, agencies, authors, and organizations for permission to use copyrighted poems, stories, and illustrations in this volume. Full illustration acknowledgments appear on page 298.

Bangs, John Kendrick: stanzas one, five, and six of "My Dog" from *Foothills of Parnassus* by John Kendrick Bangs

Bobbs-Merrill Company, Inc., The, : "Ajax" abridged from *Ajax, Golden Dog of the Australian Bush*, copyright © 1953 by Mary Elwyn Patchett, published by The Bobbs-Merrill Company, Inc. and Lutterworth Press, reprinted by permission of The Bobbs-Merrill Company, Inc. and the William Morris Agency, Inc.

Chatto and Windus, Ltd.: "The Lone Dog" from *Songs to Save a Soul* by Irene R. McLeod, courtesy of Chatto and Windus and the author's literary estate

David Higham Associates, Limited: "Dog" from *Silver Sand & Snow* by Eleanor Farjeon, published by Michael Joseph

Walt Disney Productions: Illustration (page 157) from "Lady and the Tramp," © Walt Disney Productions

Doubleday & Company, Inc.: "Why Dogs and Cats Are Not Friends" from *Wonder Tales of Dogs and Cats* by Frances Carpenter, copyright © 1955 by Frances Huntington, reprinted by permission of Doubleday & Company, Inc.; the first three stanzas of "The Animal Store," copyright 1926 by Doubleday & Company, Inc., from the book *Taxis and Toadstools* by Rachel Field, reprinted by permission of Doubleday & Company, Inc. and World's Work, Ltd.; "Bingo Has an Enemy" from *Gay Go Up* by Rose Fyleman, copyright 1929, 1930 by Doubleday & Company, Inc., reprinted by permission of Doubleday & Company, Inc. and The Society of Authors as the literary representative of the Estate of Rose Fyleman; stanzas two and four of "The Power of the Dog," copyright 1909 by Rudyard Kipling, from the book *Rudyard Kipling's Verse, Definitive Edition*, reprinted by permission of The Executors of the Estate of Mrs. George (Elsie) Bambridge, Doubleday & Company, Inc., and The Macmillan Company of London and Basingstoke

Field Enterprises, Inc.: Illustration from "Rivets" by George Sixta, © Field Enterprises, Inc., 1976

Follett Publishing Company: "Jack-in-the-Pulpit," an abridgement of the story "Someday" from *Lynn Hall's Dog Stories* by Lynn Hall, copyright © 1972 by Lynn Hall, used by permission of Follett Publishing Company

Grosset & Dunlap, Inc.: Illustration (page 141) from the book *Call of the Wild* by Jack London, special contents of this edition copyright © 1965 by Grosset & Dunlap, Inc., used by permission of the publisher

Guiterman, Vida L.: "The Dog's Cold Nose" from *Lyric Laughter* by Arthur Guiterman, © 1959 by E. P. Dutton, renewed by Vida Lindo Guiterman

Harper & Row, Publishers: Illustration of the book *Sounder* by William Armstrong

Holiday House, Inc.: "Smudgie" adapted from *Dog Story* by Oren Lyons, copyright © 1973 by Oren Lyons, reprinted by permission of Holiday House, Inc.

Holt, Rinehart and Winston: Illustration (page 141) of the book *Lassie Come-Home* by Eric Knight

Kipp, Hilda W.: "Little Puppy" from *Navajo Indian Poems* by Hilda Faunce Wetherill

J. B. Lippincott Company: Illustration (page 141) of the book *Wilderness Champion* by Joseph Lippincott

Little, Brown and Company: "The Coming of Mutt" adapted from *The Dog Who Wouldn't Be* by Farley Mowat, copyright © 1957 by the Curtis Publishing Company, copyright © 1957 by Farley Mowat, reprinted by permission of Little, Brown and Co. in association with the Atlantic Monthly Press and The Canadian Publishers, McClelland and Stewart, Limited, Toronto

Macmillan Publishing Co., Inc.: "The Hairy Dog" from *Pillicock Hill* by Herbert Asquith, reprinted with permission of Macmillan Publishing Co., Inc. and Michael Asquith; published in the United States by Macmillan Publishing Co., Inc.

McGowen, Tom: "Four Legs," copyright © 1974 by Thomas E. McGowen

William Morrow & Company, Inc.: "Ribsy and the Apartment House" adapted from *Ribsy* by Beverly Cleary, copyright © 1964 by Beverly Cleary, by permission of William Morrow & Company, Inc.

Rainbird Publishing Group, Ltd.: Illustration (pages 142-143) of Anubis from the tomb of Tutankhamen, Egyptian Museum, Cairo (F. L. Kenett, © Rainbird Publishing Group, Ltd.)

United Features Syndicate, Inc.: Illustration (pages 156-157) of "Peanuts" by Charles Schulz © 1976 by United Feature Syndicate, Inc.

The Viking Press: Illustration (page 141) of the book *The Hundred and One Dalmatians* by Dodie Smith

Contents

Preface

People have trained and made pets of many kinds of animals. But the very first animal that was trained to live with and help people—the first animal to be *domesticated*—was the dog.

The one thing that makes dogs different from all other domesticated animals is that dogs adopted people, rather than the other way around. And dogs have stayed with people—not because they were made to, but because they *wanted* to. Why? No one really knows. But there's a delightful old story that tells how dogs first chose to be with people. It goes like this:

In the beginning, Adam and Eve and all the animals lived together happily. But when Adam and Eve sinned, God was very angry. He caused a great crack to open up in the earth, separating Adam and Eve from all the animals.

The dog, of course, was on the side of the crack with the other animals. He watched anxiously as the crack yawned wider, separating him from the two people he had grown to love. Suddenly, he could stand it no longer. He gave a tremendous leap that carried him over the widening gulf and brought him down on the other side, right at the feet of Adam and Eve! And ever since, the dog has been a faithful friend and loyal comrade to people.

Here, then, is a book about these wonderful creatures we call dogs. It's about purebred dogs and mutts, about heroic dogs and famous dogs, about working dogs and show dogs. It's about dogs in myths and legends, dogs in books and art, and dogs in sayings. And it's about picking out a dog, training it, taking care of it, and—most of all—loving it.

Whether I'm Alsatian,
        Dachshund or Dalmatian,
Or any one among the Terrier crew,
        However brief you've known me,
        As long as you will own me
I'm Dog, that's all, my Master, Dog to you.

        If you like a Setter
        Or a Spaniel better,
Aberdeen or Airedale—some folks do—
        Whatever breed you name me,
        As long as you will claim me
I'm yours for life, my Master, Dog to you.

        I'll love you, Cairn or Collie,
        Beyond the point of folly,
And if I'm Mongrel, love you just as true;
        Kick me or caress me,
        As long as you possess me
I'm yours till death, my Master, Dog to you.

        For you, I'll be so knowing!
        I'll whimper at your going,
And at your coming, wag myself in two!
        Trust you while I tease you,
        Pester you to please you,
Your Dog, that's all, Master, Dog to you.

Dog
Eleanor Farjeon

1

What is a dog?

A dog is
four furry paws,
two bright eyes,
and a wet tongue...

10

...A dog is
a tail that's always moving,
an ever curious, searching nose,
and an ear cocked up
for all the sounds of the world...

...A dog is
a flashing streak
of fun on the run,
and a flop-eared pooch
snoozing on a chair...

...A dog is
one enormous appetite
that never quite gets enough,
and perfect contentment
crunching on a bone...

...A dog is
a dirt-slinging digger,
a fun-loving clown,
a sad-eyed bundle of sympathy...

...And every dog is
born to be
somebody's friend!

My dog's so furry I've not seen
His face for years and years:
His eyes are buried out of sight,
I only guess his ears.

When people ask me for his breed,
I do not know or care:
He has the beauty of them all
Hidden beneath his hair.

The Hairy Dog
Herbert Asquith

2

Curbstone setters and
blue-ribbon winners

The coming of Mutt

by Farley Mowat

If there was one drawback to life in Saskatoon, it was that we had no dog. During my lifetime we had owned, or had been owned by, a steady succession of dogs. There had always been dogs during my first eight years, until we moved to the west and became, for the moment, dogless. The prairies could be only half real to a boy without a dog.

I began agitating for one almost as soon as we arrived and I found a willing ally in my father— though his motives were not mine.

For many years he had been exposed to the colorful tales of my Great-uncle Frank, who homesteaded in Alberta in 1900. Frank was a hunter born, and most of his stories dealt with the superlative shooting to be had on the western plains. Before we were properly settled in Saskatoon my father determined to test those tales. He bought a fine English shotgun, a shooting coat, cases of ammunition, a copy of the *Saskatchewan Game Laws,* and a handbook on shotgun shooting. There remained only one indispensable item—a hunting dog.

One evening he arrived home with such a beast in tow behind him. Its name was Crown Prince Challenge Indefatigable. It stood about as high as the dining-room table and, as far as Mother and I could judge, consisted mainly of feet and tongue. Father haughtily informed us that the Crown Prince was an Irish setter, kennel bred and field trained, and a dog to delight the heart of any expert. We remained unimpressed. Purebred he may have been, and the possessor of innumerable cups and ribbons,

but to my eyes he seemed a singularly useless
sort of beast with but one redeeming feature. I
greatly admired the way he drooled. I have never
known a dog who could drool as the Crown Prince
could. He never stopped, except to flop his way
to the kitchen sink and tank-up on water. He left
a wet and sticky trail wherever he went. He had
little else to recommend him, for he was moronic.

Mother might have overlooked his obvious
defects, had it not been for his price. She could
not overlook that, for the owner was asking two
hundred dollars, and we could no more afford
such a sum than we could have afforded a
Cadillac. Crown Prince left the next morning,
but Father was not discouraged, and it was clear
that he would try again.

Mother realized that a dog was now inevitable.
When chance brought the duck boy—as we

afterwards referred to him—to our door on that August day, Mother snatched the initiative right out of my father's hands.

In our small house on the outskirts of the city my mother was preparing luncheon for my father and for me. Father had not yet returned from his office, nor I from school. The sound of the doorbell brought her unwillingly from the kitchen into the hall. She opened the front door.

A small boy, perhaps ten years of age, stood shuffling his feet. He held a wicker basket before him and, as the door opened, he swung the basket forward and spoke.

"Missus," he asked in a pale, high tone, "would you want to buy a duck?"

Mother looked into the basket and to her astonishment beheld three ducklings, their bills gaping in the heat, and, wedged between them, a nondescript and bedraggled pup.

She was touched, and curious—although she certainly did not want to buy a duck.

"I don't think so," she said kindly. "Why are you selling them?"

The boy took courage and returned her smile.

"I gotta," he said. "The slough out to the farm is dry. We ate the big ducks, but these was too small to eat. I sold some. You want the rest, lady? They're cheap—only a dime each."

"I'm sorry," Mother replied. "I've no place to keep a duck. But where did you get the dog?"

The boy shrugged his shoulders. "Oh, *him*," he said without much interest. "He was kind of an accident, you might say. I guess somebody dumped him out of a car right by our gate. I brung him with me in case. But dogs is hard to sell." He brightened up a little as an idea struck him. "Say, lady, you want him? I'll sell him for a nickel—that way you'll *save* a nickel."

Mother hesitated. Then almost involuntarily her hand went to the basket. The pup was thirsty beyond thirst, and those outstretched fingers must have seemed to him as fountains straight from heaven. He clambered hastily over the ducks and grabbed.

The boy was quick to sense his advantage and to press it home.

"He likes you, lady, see? He's yours for just *four* cents!"

By buying the duck boy's pup, Mother not only placed herself in a position to prevent the purchase of an expensive dog of my father's choice but she was also able to save six cents in cash. She was never one to despise a bargain.

When I came home from school the bargain was installed in a soap carton in the kitchen. He looked to be a somewhat dubious buy at any price. Small, very thin, and caked liberally with cow manure, he peered up at me in a nearsighted sort of way. But when I knelt beside him and extended an exploratory hand he roused himself and sank his puppy teeth into my thumb with such satisfactory gusto that my doubts dissolved. I knew that he and I would get along.

My father's reaction was of a different kind.

He arrived home at six o'clock that night and he was hardly in the door before he began singing the praises of a springer-spaniel bitch he had just seen. He seemed hardly even to hear at first when Mother interrupted to remark that we had a dog, and that two would be too many.

When he beheld the pup he was outraged; but the ambush had been well and truly laid. Before he could recover, Mother unmasked her guns.

"Isn't he *lovely,* darling?" she asked sweetly. "And so *cheap.* Do you know, I've actually saved you a hundred and ninety-nine dollars and ninety-six cents? Enough to pay for all your ammunition and for that *expensive* new gun you bought."

My father was game, and he rallied quickly. He pointed scornfully at the pup, and in a voice sharp with exasperation he replied:

"But—that—that 'thing' isn't a *hunting* dog!"

Mother was ready for him. "How do you *know,* dear," she asked, "until you've tried him out?"

There could be no adequate reply to this. It

was as impossible to predict what the pup might grow up to be, as it was to deduce what his ancestry might have been. Father turned to me for support, but I would not meet his eye, and he knew then that he had been outmaneuvered.

He accepted defeat with his usual good grace. I can clearly remember, and with awe, what he had to say to some friends who dropped in not three evenings later. The pup, relatively clean, and already beginning to fatten out a little, was presented to the guests.

"He's imported," Father explained in a modest tone of voice. "I understand he's the only one of his kind in the west. A Prince Albert retriever, you know. Marvelous breed for upland shooting."

Unwilling to confess their ignorance, the guests looked vaguely knowing. "What do you call him?" one of them asked.

I put my foot in it then. Before Father could reply, I said, "I call him Mutt." I was horrified by the look my father gave me. He turned his back on me and smiled confidentially at the guests.

"You have to be rather careful with these highly bred specimens," he explained, "it doesn't always do to let them know their kennel names. Better to give them a simple name like Sport, or Nipper, or—" and here he gagged a trifle—"or even Mutt."

About the author   Farley Mowat was born and grew up in Canada. In *The Dog Who Wouldn't Be,* from which this story was taken, he tells of his boyhood on the Canadian prairie and the dog, Mutt, who shared that time with him. You may want to read some of his other books, such as *Owls in the Family* or *The Curse of the Viking Grave.*

Crossbreds and purebreds

Have you ever heard of a dog called a Doodle? That's what you might call a dog that is half *Dachshund* and half *Poodle*—a dog who's mother was a Dachshund and whose father was a Poodle.

What would such a dog look like? Well, it might have the long body and short legs of a Dachshund and the frizzy fur of a Poodle. Or, it might have a Poodle's body and a Dachshund's head. The dog would be a *mixture* of the two dogs that were its parents. It would look a bit like both of them, but not exactly like either one of them.

And that's what a crossbred, or random-bred dog is--a mixture of two kinds of dogs, or even of many kinds of dogs. If an Irish Setter is mated with a Collie, their puppies will be half Irish Setter and half Collie. And if, when the puppies grow up, one of them is mated with a dog that is half German Shepherd and half Chow Chow, *their* puppies will be a mixture of Irish Setter, Collie, German Shepherd, and Chow Chow.

Dogs that are all mixed up like this are called mongrels, which means "of mixed breed." People call such dogs "mutts," or "pooches," or, jokingly, "curbstone setters." But mongrels are just as lovable and just as smart (maybe even smarter) than the kinds of dogs called purebreds.

And what is a purebred? Well, a purebred puppy is one whose parents are both the *same* kind of dog. This means that when the puppy grows up, it will look almost exactly like its parents. For example, if two Golden Retrievers have puppies, their puppies will all be Golden Retrievers, too. Purebreds are simply dogs that have been bred to look the same for hundreds, or even thousands, of years.

But, every kind of purebred dog started out as

The Cocker Spaniel (above) and the standard Poodle (right) are purebred dogs. They look just like their parents. The crossbred dog (below) is a mixture. It is called a Cockapoo because it is part Cocker and part Poodle. But, as you can see, it doesn't look very much like either one of its parents.

There's no doubt that these puppies belong to this proud Saint Bernard. Even their markings match.

This slender Borzoi and her look-alike pup even pose alike.

Only four weeks old, these furry little Chesapeake Bay Retriever puppies already look like their mother.

a mongrel! Every kind of purebred dog was at one time a crossbred dog. For example, the purebred dog called a Boston Terrier came about when someone mated an English Bulldog and an English Terrier. The puppies were mixtures of Bulldog and Terrier. And that's how a purebred kind of dog begins. Then, during many years, the best dogs in different litters are mated. In time, the dogs that are born look just the way the breeders want them to look.

Most of the dogs you will be reading about in this book are purebreds. But whether your dog is a purebred or a crossbred, remember that *every* kind of dog is really a mixture of two or more breeds. And every dog, of whatever kind, can be a loyal and loving friend!

The American Kennel Club, or AKC, registers 122 breeds of dogs. These breeds are divided into six groups: Sporting Dogs, Hounds, Working Dogs, Terriers, Toy Dogs, and Nonsporting Dogs. There is also a Miscellaneous Class for a few other breeds in which there is interest.

On the following pages, you can find out more about the breeds in each of these groups.

Whether your dog is a pooch or a purebred, it will give you all its love.

English Setter

Pointer

Dogs that hunt birds

Have you ever seen a dog take off lickety-split after a rabbit or a squirrel? Dogs do this because they are born with a hunting instinct. Many of the breeds in the six AKC groups are hunters.

The breeds in the Sporting Group are hunters that have been bred to find birds, get them into the air, and bring back the ones that are shot. Each breed is especially good at one or more of these jobs. The test of a good bird dog is in the field. There the dogs are judged by how well they do their job.

Pointers and setters, for instance, are very good at finding birds. It is a thrilling sight to see a Pointer going back and forth across a field, always heading into the wind so as to catch the faintest scent of a bird.

Suddenly, a frightened rabbit dashes off. But the Pointer pays no attention. His job is to hunt birds—he has no time to play. On he goes, nose high, sniffing the air. Then he freezes in his tracks, often "pointing" with one foreleg lifted. The hunter comes up, flushes the bird into the air, and fires. On command, the Pointer finds and retrieves the bird.

Sporting Group

American Water Spaniel
Brittany Spaniel
Chesapeake Bay
   Retriever
Clumber Spaniel
Cocker Spaniel
Curly-Coated Retriever
English Cocker Spaniel
English Setter
English Springer Spaniel
Field Spaniel
Flat-Coated Retriever
German Shorthaired
   Pointer
German Wirehaired
   Pointer
Golden Retriever
Gordon Setter
Irish Setter
Irish Water Spaniel
Labrador Retriever
Pointer
Sussex Spaniel
Vizsla
Weimaraner
Welsh Springer Spaniel
Wirehaired Pointing
   Griffon

For more information about these breeds, see *Dogs to know,* pages 274-292, and the Index.

Spaniels, as you might guess, came from Spain originally. These dogs do not work in quite the same way as pointers and setters. A spaniel, such as an English Springer Spaniel, works close to the hunter, with its nose near the ground. It does not stop and point when it smells a bird. Instead, the spaniel goes into the bushes and springs, or flushes, the bird into the air. On command, the spaniel then races to retrieve it.

English Springer Spaniel

Chesapeake Bay Retriever

As you can guess from the name, retrievers have been bred to retrieve, or bring back, the birds. Retrievers are not usually expected to point or to flush. They are trained to heel—to stay by the hunter's side—until commanded to make the retrieve.

Retrievers work well on land, but water is their specialty. And the weather matters not. It can be freezing cold, with a strong, gusty wind whipping up the waves. But on the command, "Fetch!" the retriever will leap into the water. Swimming strongly, it will find the bird and make the retrieve. And it will hold the bird so gently, there won't be a toothmark!

By sight and scent

The dogs in the Hound Group all hunt by sight or scent. The breed name often tells you what kind of animal a hound is bred to hunt.

Both the American Foxhound and the English Foxhound were bred to hunt foxes. These dogs work in packs and hunt by scent. As the hounds trail the fox across the countryside, they are followed by red-coated hunters on horseback. Of course, the hounds are supposed to catch and kill the fox. For this reason, many people think that this is a cruel kind of sport that should be stopped.

Another kind of fox hunt—one that spares the fox—is the drag hunt. Before the drag hunt, a fox-scented sack is dragged over the trail. The hounds then follow the fresh scent.

The night hunt is another kind of fox hunt, one that is a contest between the fox and the hounds.

English Foxhounds

Black and Tan Coonhound

Basenji

While the hounds chase the fox, the "hunters" sit around a campfire. The baying of the hounds enables them to follow every move in the contest. When the fox goes into its burrow, the dogs are called in. The fox is left to run another night.

Coonhounds use their keen sense of smell to hunt raccoons. They can also be trained to hunt other animals. The AKC registers only the Black and Tan Coonhound. The American Coonhunters Association keeps a studbook for other breeds, such as the Redbone Hound, the Plott Hound, and the Bluetick Coonhound.

Many hounds, such as the Coonhound, Basset Hound, and Bloodhound have long, floppy ears. These long ears have a purpose. When a scent hound goes back and forth, nose to the ground, its long, floppy ears stir up bits of scent.

But not all hounds have long, floppy ears. The Norwegian Elkhound, bred to hunt the elk, and the Basenji, the barkless dog from Africa, don't look like most hounds. Both breeds have short, pointy ears and a curly tail.

Hounds that hunt by sight include the fastest, tallest, and oldest breeds in the world. All are members of the Greyhound family.

The Greyhound, the fastest of all dogs, has been timed at a speed of more than forty miles (64 kilometers) per hour. The gentle, intelligent Irish Wolfhound, famous for its ability to chase down wolves, is the tallest of all dogs. It stands about 32 inches (81 centimeters) high.

The slender Saluki is thought to be the oldest purebred dog. It is also one of the swiftest dogs. This beautiful, graceful dog enjoys a special place of honor in the Arab world. Most Arabs are Moslems. In their religion, dogs are considered unclean. But the Saluki was so important to them, they declared it sacred and called it "the noble one" given to them by God.

Irish Wolfhound

Bernese Mountain Dog

Helping paws

The dogs in the Working Group were all bred to help people in their work. You might say that these dogs "lend a helping paw."

A working dog must be strong and hardy, able to do all kinds of work in all kinds of weather. The Bernese Mountain Dog is a good example of a working dog. This handsome, long-haired dog first gained attention as a draft dog, pulling small wagons and carts. The Bernese comes from the Canton of Berne in Switzerland. For many years, the basket weavers of Berne used these dogs to haul their wares to market.

Swiss farmers also used the Bernese to cart milk, fruit, and vegetables over steep mountain trails to busy market places. At one time it was a common sight to see these big dogs at work. Even today, you may still see a Bernese hitched to a small wagon. But most are now kept as pets.

The German Shepherd dog, or Alsatian as it is known in England, is a working dog that might well be called a jack of all trades. This dog was first bred in Germany as a sheep dog. When there was less need for shepherd dogs, this fine animal was trained as a police dog. During World War I, German Shepherd Dogs found wounded

Working Group

Akita
Alaskan Malamute
Bearded Collie
Belgian Malinois
Belgian Sheepdog
Belgian Tervuren
Bernese Mountain Dog
Bouvier des Flandres
Boxer
Briard
Bullmastiff
Cardigan Welsh Corgi
Collie
Doberman Pinscher
German Shepherd Dog
Giant Schnauzer
Great Dane
Great Pyrenees
Komondor
Kuvasz
Mastiff
Newfoundland
Old English Sheepdog
Pembroke Welsh Corgi
Puli
Rottweiler
Saint Bernard
Samoyed
Shetland Sheepdog
Siberian Husky
Standard Schnauzer

For more information about these breeds, see *Dogs to know*, pages 274-292, and the Index.

39

Puli

soldiers and worked as guards and messengers on the battlefield. After the war, these dogs took on still another job—as guide dogs for the blind. And more than one has been a star in the movies and on television.

For many years, the Alaskan Malamute and the Siberian Husky were the hard working dogs of the North. Teams of these dogs are sometimes still used to pull sleds loaded with supplies. Both breeds have thick, heavy coats that protect them from the bitter Arctic cold.

Another mighty working dog is the big Saint Bernard. You can read about Barry, the most famous of these dogs, on pages 112-113.

Sheep dogs and cattle dogs are bred to help as herders. Sometimes when a sheep runs away, the Puli, a sheep dog from Hungary, jumps on the sheep's back and rides it until the sheep is tired. Then the Puli herds the sheep back to the flock.

A real hero among working dogs is the huge, powerful Newfoundland. Newfoundlands are strong swimmers and have saved countless people from drowning at sea. And in Newfoundland, this dog's island home, the sturdy Newfoundland can still be seen pulling carts and carrying things on its back like a pack horse.

But in most places, the Newfoundland is kept as a companion and children's pet. Maybe that's why James Barrie chose a Newfoundland to be the nursemaid in his story, *Peter Pan*.

Newfoundland (Landseer, or black and white, variety)

*Dandie
Dinmont
Terrier*

Digger dogs

For more information about
these breeds, see *Dogs to know*,
pages 274-292, and the Index

Terra is the Latin word for earth, and that's
where the name "terrier" comes from. Terriers
are truly "earth dogs." These brave, scrappy
dogs were bred to follow small animals into their
underground burrows.

The Cairn Terrier is the smallest of the many
terriers bred in Scotland. It takes its name from
piles of stones called cairns. A fearless hunter,
the Cairn is famous for its ability to squeeze into
small spaces between rocks as it goes after foxes
and rodents.

Another breed of Scottish terrier got its name
from Sir Walter Scott, one of Scotland's greatest
writers. In one of his books, Scott told about a
farmer who had six terriers, known as Mustard
and Pepper Terriers because of their coloring.
The Farmer called his dogs Little Pepper, Young
Pepper, Auld (old) Pepper, Little Mustard, Young
Mustard, and Auld Mustard.

Many readers enjoyed Scott's story and were
interested in the fearless little terriers. What's

Cairn Terrier

more, people gave these dogs the name of the farmer in the story—Dandie Dinmont. And that's the name they've had ever since.

The Bull Terrier was bred in England as a fighting dog. Today, the "sport" of dog fighting is against the law in most countries. But this strong, brave, and friendly dog has found favor as a watchdog and pet. With its oval-shaped face and alert, upright ears, the Bull Terrier looks like a no-nonsense dog. The coat is either all white or colored.

Another English terrier, the Airedale Terrier, is the largest of all terriers. First used to hunt small game, the plucky Airedale has proven a match for mountain lions and wolves.

The Airedale has also done well in police work and as an alert guard and messenger during wars.

Bull Terrier

Airedale Terrier

Australian Terrier

Manchester Terrier

A loyal companion and watchdog, the Airedale is very good around children.

One of the smallest and newest of terriers comes from the other side of the world. It's the Australian Terrier. Developed less than a hundred years ago, these spunky little dogs have tended sheep, guarded mines, and been used by farmers to hunt snakes and rats. Surprisingly quiet for a terrier, the little Australian is a favorite housedog in many parts of the world.

Pug and puppy

Small, smaller, smallest

If you have a Toy dog, or know a person who has one, then you know that these little dogs are not "toys." Small as they are, the dogs in the Toy Group are not playthings. These dogs are called Toys because of their size.

The Pug may be one of the oldest of the small breeds with a pushed-up face. Traders brought this little dog from China about four hundred years ago. It soon became a darling of the ladies at many of the courts of Europe. About fifty years ago, however, the Pug went out of fashion and almost disappeared. Fortunately, it did not disappear. These affectionate "little dogs with dirty faces" are still with us.

The smallest of all dogs is the tiny Chihuahua. These dogs are named for the Mexican state where American tourists found them more than a hundred years ago. Many people think the breed is Mexican, but the Chihuahua was known in Europe as much as five hundred years ago. However, the Chihuahua we know today was developed in the United States.

Long ago, Toy dogs were kept only by royalty or the very rich. The common people couldn't afford to keep dogs just as pets. Their dogs had to earn their keep.

In ancient China, the Pekingese was a highly treasured possession of emperors and considered sacred. These dogs were seldom seen outside the palace grounds. The punishment for stealing one of them was death.

Another favorite pet of Chinese royalty was the Shih Tzu (sheed zoo), which means "lion's son." And in Chinese art, this small, long-haired Toy dog does look like the king of beasts.

The Japanese Spaniel, or Chin as it is known in

Toy Group

Affenpinscher
Brussels Griffon
Chihuahua
English Toy Spaniel
Italian Greyhound
Japanese Spaniel
Maltese
Manchester Terrier (Toy)
Miniature Pinscher
Papillon
Pekingese
Pomeranian
Poodle (Toy)
Pug
Shih Tzu
Silky Terrier
Yorkshire Terrier

For more information about these breeds, see *Dogs to know,* pages 274-292, and the Index.

Papillon

Japan, was long a royal favorite in that country. These dogs became known to the rest of the world when some were given as gifts to important people from other countries.

It is no accident that some Toys look like small copies of other breeds. Five hundred years ago, spaniels were a very popular hunting dog. But these dogs, often muddy from a day in the field, didn't appeal to the ladies. So, breeders set about developing a dwarf spaniel that would be a good lap dog. At first, this new breed of dogs had large, drooping ears. For some unknown reason,

Italian Greyhound

Shih Tzu

the present type, with stand-up ears, was developed later. Because of the appearance of the ears, the French gave the breed the name *Papillon,* meaning "butterfly."

Men, as well as women, have been charmed by the Toy breeds. More than two hundred years ago, Frederick the Great was king of Prussia. When he rode off to war, he took along his favorite dog, an Italian Greyhound, in his saddlebag. These little dogs look like, and are, miniature Greyhounds.

There are other look-alikes among the Toys and the larger dogs. The Miniature Pinscher might easily be mistaken for the bigger Doberman Pinscher, although it is a much older breed than the Doberman. And the Toy Manchester Terrier and the Toy Poodle both have look-alikes. But neither of these Toys is considered a separate breed. In general, each must meet the same standards as its bigger cousin.

Small as they are, the Toys are very good watchdogs. Their shrill barks often serve to frighten away would-be robbers. And many of these dogs can appear to be very fierce.

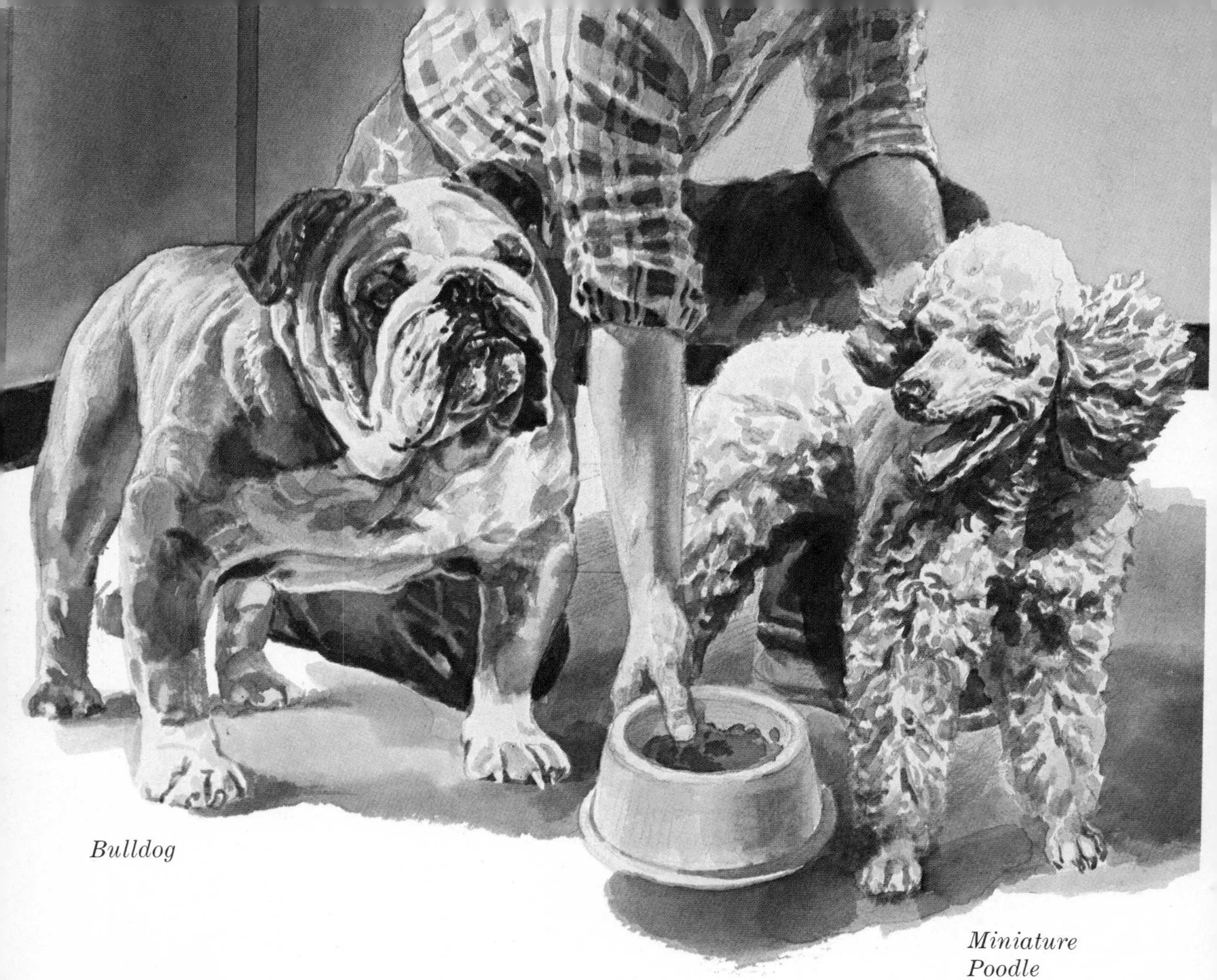

Bulldog

Miniature Poodle

Companion dogs

Nonsporting Group

Bichon Frise
Boston Terrier
Bulldog
Chow Chow
Dalmatian
French Bulldog
Keeshond
Lhasa Apso
Poodle
Schipperke
Tibetan Terrier

For more information about these breeds, see *Dogs to know,* pages 274-292, and the Index.

The dogs in the Nonsporting Group are now generally bred as pets or, as many people prefer to think of them, companion dogs. But, like most dogs, many were first bred for other reasons.

The friendly, good-natured Bulldog is the national dog of England. It is also the mascot of the British Navy and of Yale University. The Bulldog has long been a symbol standing for the idea of holding on, of not giving up.

Bulldogs were first bred for the "sport" of bull-baiting. In this once-popular pastime, the dog was set after a bull that was tied to a line

Chow Chow

attached to a stake. The dog would charge in and grab the bull by its tender nose, then the dog would hang on until the bull went down on its knees. Happily, this terrible and cruel "sport" was outlawed long ago.

Perhaps you've wondered why the Bulldog's lower jaw sticks out and its nose is pushed back. The Bulldog was bred this way so that it could breathe more easily while hanging on to the bull.

One of the most popular companion dogs is the bright, fun-loving Poodle. These intelligent dogs are also used in many dog acts because they are wonderful performers. But the Poodle was not always a pet or a performing dog. In spite of its fancy appearance, the Poodle was first bred as a water retriever.

Many people think the Poodle is the national dog of France. It's not, though it has long been a favorite in that country. In fact, lots of people call this dog a French Poodle. But the French call the Poodle *Caniche.* This name is short for *chien canard,* meaning "duck dog." And in France, this dog was used to retrieve ducks.

The Poodle, however, probably comes from Germany, not from France. The English name *Poodle* comes from the German *Pudelhund.* *Pudeln* means "to splash water" and *hund* means "dog." So *Poodle* means "splash dog."

Poodles come in three different sizes: Standard, Miniature, and Toy. The Standard is the largest and the oldest. The other sizes were developed from the Standard. Both the Standard and the Miniature are in the Nonsporting Group. The Toy, of course, is in the Toy Group.

The Chow Chow, or just Chow as it is usually called, comes from China, where it was used as a hunting dog. The name *Chow* comes from a Chinese word that means "dog." The Chow Chow is the only breed of dog with a blue-black tongue.

Schipperke

Dalmatian

Today, the spotted Dalmatian is often a mascot at a firehouse. Here's why. The Dalmatian is born with a love for horses, so it's not surprising that it became best known as a coach dog. These dogs once ran alongside or under horse-drawn coaches and carriages. Sometimes they even ran between the horses. Their job was to chase away dogs, act as a guard, and serve as a decoration.

When firemen began to use horse-drawn fire engines, they often had Dalmatians to keep dogs and people away from the horses and equipment. And so, though the horses are gone from the firehouse, the Dalmatian is still there. But now it is a pet and mascot.

The Bichon Frise (BEE shahn free ZAY) was a favorite of Spanish, French, and Italian royalty. Henry III, who was king of France four hundred years ago, was very fond of these little dogs. He used to carry them around with him in a traylike basket suspended from his neck with ribbons. Later, the Bichon became a street dog, trained to entertain at fairs and circuses.

Bichon Frise

Ibizan Hound

Border Collie

Up-and-coming breeds

There are hundreds of breeds of dogs in the world. No kennel club registers all breeds. As of 1977, the American Kennel Club, or AKC, registers only 122 breeds.

Dogs of these 122 breeds can be registered in the AKC Stud Book, which is a book that gives pedigrees and performance records. Each year, the names of more than a million dogs are added to the book. This book now contains the names and records of more than eighteen million dogs!

But what about other breeds? Will the AKC ever register any of them? The chances are that the AKC will register some. In fact, in 1976, the Bearded Collie was the latest breed to be admitted to the AKC Stud Book.

To provide a step toward such admission, the AKC maintains a Miscellaneous Class for dogs of

up-and-coming breeds. When there is proof of
wide interest and activity in a breed, that breed
may be admitted to the Miscellaneous Class. This
breed may then compete in AKC obedience trials
and earn obedience titles. It can also compete in
the Miscellaneous Class at shows, but cannot
earn championship points. At the present time,
there are seven breeds in the Miscellaneous Class.

For a breed to make it into the AKC Stud Book,
many people must be interested in owning and
working with dogs of that breed. There must be
a number of breeders and at least one breed club.
And everyone must agree on what a perfect dog
of that breed should look like.

Spinoni Italiani

*Cavalier King
Charles Spaniel*

Miniature Bull Terrier

Dogs around the world

If you want a dog that's different—one that's not like any dog on your block—there are lots of breeds to choose from. But you might find it very difficult—and expensive—to get hold of most of these breeds. That's because they are seldom seen outside their own countries.

Most of us know only the kinds of dogs we see every day. You'd almost certainly know a Collie. But what about an Armant, an Hellenic Hound, or a Polski Ogar?

If you lived in Egypt, you'd probably know the Armant. These strong, long-haired dogs have been used there as guard dogs and sheep dogs for many, many years.

If you lived in Greece, you might know the Hellenic Hound. *Hellenic* means "Greek," and this medium-sized hound is a hunting dog with a keen nose.

What about the Polski Ogar? Can you guess where this breed is best known? The first word, Polski, might give you a clue. If you haven't guessed, the name means "Polish Hound." And in Poland, this hunting dog has been a favorite for years because it is at home in all kinds of weather.

The Tosa, or Japanese Fighting Dog, is now a favorite family dog in Japan. But the Tosa was first bred for dog fights, which are now outlawed. Today, these dogs are usually companion or guard dogs. The Tosa takes its name from the province of Tosa. In Japan, it is known as the *Tosa Inu,* or Tosa Dog.

A sailor with a lot of experience is often called a "sea dog." And that would be a good name for the Portuguese Water Dog. These animals have been going to sea for years. Many are regular crew members on Portuguese fishing boats. The

Tosa Inu, or Tosa Dog

dogs are used to retrieve fish, nets, and ropes from the sea. They are excellent swimmers, and sometimes carry messages between boats. When their ships are in port, the dogs serve as guards.

Many of the breeds not registered by the AKC are registered by the kennel clubs in other countries. The clubs of France, Germany, and The Netherlands were the first to register the Leonberger. This powerful dog, named after the

Canaan Dog

Jack Russell Terrier

city of Leonberg, Germany, pulls carts and
protects farm animals. Basically, it was bred
from two huge working dogs—the Saint Bernard
and the Newfoundland. Later, other breeds, such
as the Great Pyrenees and various sheep dogs,
were added to the breeding. The result was a
huge dog with a long, golden coat.

Have you ever heard of the Canaan Dog, the
national dog of Israel? An intelligent dog, it has
been used in war and as a guide dog for the blind.
This dog from the Biblical "Land of Canaan" is
registered by the kennel clubs of Great Britain,
Canada, Mexico, and a few other countries.

Portuguese Water Dog

There is a type of terrier, long popular in England, that isn't registered anywhere as a breed. It is the Jack Russell Terrier, named for the man who helped form the Kennel Club in England more than a hundred years ago. And most Jack Russell breeders don't want these dogs registered by kennel clubs. They want the Jack Russells bred as workers and companions, not as show dogs.

There's always a chance that a popular breed in one country will become popular in another country. For, as anyone who loves dogs knows, there's always room for another breed.

I'm a lean dog, a keen dog, a wild dog, and lone;
I'm a rough dog, a tough dog, hunting on my own;
I'm a bad dog, a mad dog, teasing silly sheep;
I love to sit and bay the moon, to keep fat souls from sleep.

I'll never be a lap dog, licking dirty feet,
A sleek dog, a meek dog, cringing for my meat,
Not for me the fireside, the well-filled plate,
But shut door, and sharp stone, and cuff and kick and hate.

Not for me the other dogs, running by my side,
Some have run a short while, but none of them would bide.
O mine is still the lone trail, the hard trail, the best,
Wide wind, and wild stars, and hunger of the quest!

Lone Dog
Irene Rutherford McLeod

3

Dogs through the ages

Four-Legs

by Tom McGowen

Tall-Tree had killed a fine, fat bird and was on his way back to the tribal caves when he came across the wolf cub. It was lying with the back of its body pinned among the branches of a fallen tree. There had been a storm during the night, and a howl of wind had torn the dead trunk in two and sent it crashing to the ground. The frightened cub, although unhurt, had been trapped among the branches when the tree fell.

It was a very young cub and quite small, but meat was meat. Tall-Tree lifted his spear. Then he paused. It had come to him that babies have a way of growing bigger. If he kept the cub until it grew to full size, it would provide a great deal more meat.

The thought seemed a good one, so Tall-Tree unwrapped a strip of leather that had been twined around his forearm and tied the cub's front legs together. It growled and snapped at him, but its teeth were too small to damage his tough skin. Then, Tall-Tree heaved the branches aside and yanked the cub free. It scrabbled at him furiously with its back legs until he tied them, too. Then Tall-Tree strode on his way.

Coming to the place of caves, he went to the great fire to turn over the results of his hunt as was the law. Old Bent-Leg sat before the fire, his good leg tucked beneath him. The withered one, crushed by a bison many snows ago, was stretched out. Bent-Leg kept tally on the game that young hunters brought. Tall-Tree dropped the bird on the small pile of animals near the old man's leg. Bent-Leg nodded, then jerked his head toward the wolf cub that hung from Tall-Tree's hand.

"What is that?" grunted the old hunter.

"A small four-legs night-howler," Tall-Tree replied, giving his people's name for the animal. "It came to me that I could keep it tied in my cave and feed it scraps from my own food. When it is full grown, we can kill it for its meat."

Bent-Leg frowned, but realized the cleverness of Tall-Tree's thinking.

"That is good!" he exclaimed. "It is little meat now, but it will be much meat later!"

Food was always a problem for the tribe. Daily, the men hunted for animals and birds while the women and children searched for roots, berries, and insects that could be eaten. Everything that was found was shared by the tribe, and often there was hardly enough.

Tall-Tree went to his cave. Near the entrance was a large boulder, beside which he dropped the whining, squirming cub. Then from the cave he brought several thin strips of animal hide. These he knotted together to make a rope, which he quickly tied around the cub's neck, avoiding its snapping teeth. Then, with a grunt, he tipped the boulder up and kicked the free end of the rope beneath it. Letting the boulder settle back with a thump, he untied the animal's legs.

The cub rolled to its feet, shook itself, and made a dash for freedom, only to have its legs jerked out from under it as the rope pulled it to an abrupt stop. Seeing that the four-legs was firmly tethered, Tall-Tree nodded and reentered his cave.

The midafternoon sun was high and hot when he came out later. The four-legs' head was down, its tail drooped, and it panted noisily. Tall-Tree thought that if he were the four-legs, tied in the hot sun all this time, he'd be thirsty. Unslinging the animal-skin water bag that hung over his shoulder, he untied its mouth and poured a small puddle onto the ground. The cub growled faintly, but inched forward and began to lap the water.

Tall-Tree frowned. He would often be gone for long trips, and he wondered how to keep the cub supplied with water during his absence. He did not want it to die of thirst.

He went into the cave for his sharp-edged digging stone. Outside again, he began chopping at the sandy soil. Growling, the four-legs backed away as far as the leather rope would let it, and glared at him.

In a short time, Tall-Tree had made a hole that seemed suitably deep. He lined the hole with an animal skin, weighting down the edges with small rocks. Then he emptied his water bag into the hole. The skin held the water. The four-legs now had its own water hole, which would keep it from getting thirsty. Tall-Tree grunted in approval and left.

When he returned, he carried several meaty bones, left from his share of food at the tribal fire. He dropped these before the four-legs, although it growled at him. Later, from within his cave, he could hear its teeth scraping on the bones.

Every day Tall-Tree put fresh water into the four-legs' water hole, brought it scraps of meat, and cleaned up after it. As the days passed, he noticed a change. The four-legs no longer growled at him when he came near. In fact, when it saw him coming now, it would stand and watch him, moving its tail back and forth in an odd way. Tall-Tree realized the four-legs no longer feared him. He found it pleasant to have the little animal acting friendly toward him. He was surprised to find himself talking to it as though it were a child.

"Here is your meat, Four-Legs," he would call as he approached with a handful of scraps. "Are you thirsty, Four-Legs?" he would ask as he filled its water hole. The animal's ears would twitch and its tail would move back and forth at the sound of his voice.

And Tall-Tree no longer had to guard against the cub's teeth. Instead of tossing the meat and bones to the animal, he now let the cub take them from his hand. And once, as he was filling the water hole, the four-legs pushed its nose against his hand and licked it. Tall-Tree jerked his hand back in surprise. But then, hesitantly, he held it out again. Once more the pink tongue flashed out and the bushy tail fanned the air, furiously. Tall-Tree grinned.

After that, he began to play a game with the wolf cub. Whenever he approached the cave, he would try to surprise the animal by coming from a different direction or by moving stealthily. But always, the four-legs would be staring straight at him, straining at the rope and beating the air with its tail.

Then, one day when Tall-Tree was bringing the catch from his hunting to the fire, Bent-Leg peered up at him.

"Is the four-legs fat enough?" asked Bent-Leg.

Tall-Tree hesitated. He had nearly forgotten his reason for keeping the cub.

"Not yet," he said, uncomfortably.

"But soon, eh?" queried Bent-Leg. Tall-Tree nodded and hurried away.

At his cave he squatted and looked anxiously at the wolf cub. It *had* grown, and before long it would be as big as it was going to get. Then he would have to turn it over to be meat for the tribe, as he had promised.

But he didn't want the four-legs to die. He knew that something had happened to him and to it. Perhaps because it had been so little when he found it, it had not grown up to be like other wolves that showed their teeth at men and then ran from them. Instead of being a wild animal, Four-Legs was more like a child that liked him. And he liked it!

The next day, Tall-Tree went hunting. He was determined to bring back more game than ever before. Perhaps, he thought, if he brought plenty of meat, Bent-Leg would forget about the wolf. But the hunt went badly. He returned with only a young squirrel. And, to his dismay, none of the other hunters had fared well, either. The pile of animals by the fire was smaller than usual.

"It is not enough!" said Bent-Leg. "We must have the four-legs now, Tall-Tree."

"Wait a few more days," said Tall-Tree. "The hunting may grow even harder. We may need the four-legs even more then."

Bent-Leg did not press him, so he hurried away. At his cave he knelt beside the wolf and rubbed its head. It nudged him with a cold nose and swept the ground with its tail.

That night, lying beside the fire in his cave, he knew that the next day, or the day after that, he would have to give the wolf to the tribe. Dreading the dawn, he fell asleep.

It seemed only seconds later that something suddenly awakened him. It was Four-Legs, snarling furiously.

Tall-Tree was up and on his feet in an instant. Snatching his spear, he peered over the nearly dead fire. In the moonlight Four-Legs stood before the cave, snarling and showing its teeth, its fur bristling. Beyond it, green eyes gleamed and scales glinted on a long, sinuous body. There was an evil hiss and a rattling sound. The hair at the back of Tall-Tree's neck rose as he saw the great snake, poised to sink its poisonous fangs into the wolf's body.

Tall-Tree exploded into action. Leaping over the fire, he swung his spear forward like a club, slamming it into the snake's body, just below the swaying head. The heavy blow knocked the serpent writhing to the ground. Springing after it, Tall-Tree pounded his spear on the snake's head again and again.

After a time, Tall-Tree leaned on his spear, panting heavily. Although the snake's body still feebly twisted, he knew it was dead. Four-Legs knew it was dead, too, and stopped growling.

Tall-Tree knew what had happened. Drawn by the heat of the fire, the deadly snake had crawled toward the cave. If it had been attracted by the warmth of Tall-Tree's body, it probably would have coiled itself next to him. Had he jostled it, the creature would certainly have bitten him. He recalled when just such a snake had bitten a man. The man had raved with pain, and then died. Tall-Tree shivered. If Four-Legs had not growled and wakened him, he also might have died.

Tall-Tree fed the fire until it blazed up again. Then he dragged the snake into the cave and began to skin it. When he had finished, he gazed thoughtfully at the thick coils of white meat.

At dawn, he hurried to the tribal fire, carrying the snake meat. Bent-Leg was already there, as were several hunters waiting for a lighter sky before starting on their way. Among them was Green-Leaf, the tribe's leader. Tall-Tree dumped the coils of meat near Bent-Leg's feet.

"I have meat for the tribe," he said, looking at Green-Leaf. "I will hunt for other meat this day, but I bring this meat now."

The men stared at the white coils. "Where did you find this long-crawler?" asked Green-Leaf.

"It came to my cave, seeking the warmth of the fire as long-crawlers do after sundown," Tall-Tree replied. "I killed it."

"Were you bitten?" asked Green-Leaf, looking at him anxiously.

Tall-Tree shook his head. "I might have been bitten," he said. "But the four-legs tied at my cave woke me with the noise of its anger. It saved my life." He looked into Green-Leaf's eyes. "I was going to give the four-legs as meat for the tribe. Let me give this meat instead, Green-Leaf. Let the four-legs live!"

Green-Leaf considered his words. "I do not know what an animal is good for, except to eat. What will you do with the four-legs?"

"I will set it free," answered Tall-Tree.

The chieftain thought. "It is well," he said at last. "You promised the tribe meat, and you brought meat as you promised. The four-legs saved you to hunt for the tribe. Let it go then, if that is your wish."

Tall-Tree walked slowly back to his cave. He was glad that the wolf would not have to die. Yet he felt as though a big stone sat heavily inside his chest. He knew that the moment he untied Four-Legs' rope, the wolf would run off into the forest. Tall-Tree did not like this thought, but he felt he must set Four-Legs free. It was the only way he could repay the animal for saving his life.

At the cave, he knelt, loosened the knot in the leather rope, and pulled it off Four-Legs' neck. The wolf shook itself and looked at him strangely. Tall-Tree turned and went into the cave. He felt a wetness in his eyes, something he had not felt since he was a boy. He squatted by the fire and gathered his weapons for the day's hunt.

Something pattered over the cave floor behind him. Tall-Tree turned. Four-Legs stood just inside the cave opening. Its tail drooped and it held its head low. Its brown eyes stared into Tall-Tree's black ones.

Then the animal moved into the cave. It was a strange movement. Its stomach was flat on the ground, but the back part of its body was pointed upward. It inched forward with little pulls of its front paws. Slowly, it crept toward Tall-Tree until its nose was only inches from the man's face.

Then it licked Tall-Tree's nose.

Tall-Tree yelled with delight. Four-Legs didn't want to leave; it had said so as plainly as if it could talk! Tall-Tree rubbed the animal's head with both hands. Four-Legs flopped onto its back, and Tall-Tree rubbed its stomach. The wolf's tongue lolled out of its mouth, and its lips were pulled back into what seemed to be a grin as wide as the one on Tall-Tree's face.

After a while Tall-Tree jumped to his feet. "Come, Four-Legs," he said. "Let's go hunting!"

Four-Legs rolled to its feet and shook itself. Then the world's first pet and its two-legged friend happily hurried off together.

About the author   Tom McGowen is a Senior Editor on *Childcraft* and the author of more than a dozen children's books. If you enjoyed this story, which was first published in *Cricket, the magazine for children,* you may want to read some of Tom's books, such as *Dragon Stew, Sir MacHinery, Odyssey from River Bend,* or *Spirit of the Wild.*

The first dogs

The wolf is probably the direct ancestor of the dog. If so, the first "dogs" were really wolves. How did these big, wild animals and people get to be such good friends?

Did people capture some wolves, tame them, and turn them into pets and helpers? Probably not. Some scientists think that wolves and people just got used to each other over many thousands of years. Here is how it might have happened.

Twenty thousand and more years ago, there were small groups of people living in most parts of the world. These people didn't live in towns or cities. They lived out in the open, in little huts, or in tents, or sometimes in caves. They hunted animals for most of their food, and used nearly every part of each animal they killed. They ate the meat, made the skins into clothing, and used the bones for spearpoints, drills, and needles.

But there was always something left—bones and inside parts that people didn't care to eat or couldn't use. And, of course, these people of long ago had no garbage cans or disposal units. So they simply left on the ground what they didn't eat or use.

Other creatures were always glad to get these leftovers. At night, while people slept, packs and families of wolves prowled about in search of food. They smelled the remains thrown away by people and crept in quietly to munch on all these good things.

There were always such leftovers near any camping place. And so packs of wolves got used to staying near the camps in order to enjoy free meals. At first, perhaps, people may not have liked having wild animals so near. They probably tried to drive the wolves away, and may have even killed some of them. But the wolves simply hid, and stayed close to be near the food.

In time, people probably discovered that the wolves were useful in a number of ways. If a

The two dogs living with these Australian Aborigines are Dingoes. The Dingo is a wild dog that still looks, and probably acts, much like some of the first dogs.

dangerous animal, such as a bear or a cave lion, came near, the wolves would set up a great racket of snarls that alerted people to the danger. Sometimes, the wolves may have chased a deer or other animal toward the camp. Then the men would be able to kill it easily. Gradually, people learned to put up with the wolves and stopped trying to drive them away.

As hundreds of years passed, generations of wolves and people grew up living near one another. They grew more and more used to each other. Wolf puppies that strayed close to a camp were probably picked up, played with, and fed special scraps by the children.

Many of the wolf pups stayed with the children and grew up as their pets. When the men went hunting, these grown-up wolves went along with them—and were a big help in finding, chasing, and catching animals.

And that is how, we think, some wolves slowly changed and became dogs—the friendly, loyal, tail-wagging creatures we love so much.

The oldest known dog

Dawn was breaking over the land. Within a large cave on a hillside, there was stir and bustle. The people who made the cave their home were busy getting ready for a new day.

These people were dark-haired and dark-eyed. They dressed in clothing made from the skins of animals. Each person had some kind of work to do. A group of young men, armed with spears, started out to hunt the day's meat. With them were a number of dogs—big, powerful creatures. A number of women went out into the hills to gather plants that could be eaten. Older men and some women stayed near the cave, busy at tasks of mending and making things.

The children, too, had their work. A boy and girl came out of the cave and headed for a distant clump of trees and shrubs to gather firewood. In her arms, the girl held a pudgy, excited puppy. It had been born in the cave a few weeks before. This was its first day out in the world.

As the children worked, the puppy waddled about, exploring. It found many interesting smells to sniff and follow. It discovered, with amazement, all the many different insects that scurried about in the grass. It broke into a burst of surprised barks when a flock of birds suddenly fluttered up out of a tree.

Day after day, the puppy followed the boy and girl at their tasks. As the weeks and months went by, the dog grew quickly. Soon it was a big, savage beast that could chase down an animal and kill it easily. But this dog was still the special pet of the boy and girl.

Soon, the dog joined the hunting pack. It did its job, helping the hunters find food. But when it returned after each hunt, it would rush to find its two young masters. Then it would leap upon them with a furiously wagging tail and many wet licks of its long, red tongue. And in time, the boy, who had also become big and sturdy, joined the hunters, too. Now the dog's joy was complete, for at least one master was with it at all times.

The girl and boy were a woman and a man, now. A baby girl was born to them. At first the dog sniffed at this tiny, pink thing suspiciously. But before long, the dog's tail began to wag. When the baby was old enough to reach out a hand to touch the dog's nose or grab for its ear, the dog would lick the tiny hand. And when the little one began to crawl and toddle, the dog let her clamber upon it without protest.

Winters and summers passed. Now too old and slow to hunt, the dog spent most of its time dozing in a patch of sunlight. But its masters still shared their food with it, just as all the people in the cave continued to share food with the old ones who could no longer work.

One day, the dog lay down to sleep and did not awaken again. Its life was over. Grieving, the man and woman and their little girl dug a shallow grave for their old friend. They dug the grave in the floor of the cave where they lived.

This was where they buried all their dead. In this way, it seemed that the dead ones were still with them, still sharing the cave that had been their home. And so, as they covered up the dog's body, they knew that their old friend with the wagging tail and wet, loving tongue would still be with them in their hearts.

Hundreds of years passed. The cave was now empty. People had become housebuilders and town-dwellers. Thousands of years went by. The cave became filled with dust and rubble, blown in by wind and carried in by rain. Part of the roof fell in, littering the floor with stone and earth.

These men are sitting in the cave in Iraq where the jawbone of a dog that lived 14,000 years ago was found. It is the oldest known dog.

After many more thousands of years went by, a group of scientists came to the cave. They suspected that people might once have lived there. They began to dig, slowly and carefully. They found the bones of people who had been buried in the cave. They found bits of tools and weapons. And they found the jawbone of a dog.

We don't really know, of course, what sort of life that dog had. We only know that it *did* live in that cave, with a group of prehistoric people, fourteen thousand years ago. It is the oldest known dog. Perhaps its story was much like the story we have just told.

timber wolf   *red wolf*

Mexican wolf

From a wolf to a lap dog

Some kinds of dogs still look somewhat like the wolves that were probably their ancestors. The German Shepherd Dog looks much like a wolf. So do the Alaskan Malamute, the Siberian Husky, and the Norwegian Elkhound. But a chubby, snub-nosed little Pekingese certainly doesn't look anything like a wolf. Neither does a long-bodied, short-legged Dachshund. If wolves were the first dogs, why don't *all* dogs still look like wolves? Why are some dogs so different?

Most dogs do not look like wolves because dogs have slowly changed during many thousands of years. Here's how it happened.

Wolves aren't all alike. Just as there are a great many differences among people, there are many differences among wolves. Some wolves are much smarter than others, some are much stronger, and some are much faster. Some wolves are one color and some another color. Some have long noses, some have shorter noses, and so on.

If a long-nosed wolf mates with a wolf that has a short nose, some of their puppies will have long noses and some will have short noses. But if two long-nosed wolves mate, *most* of their puppies will have long noses.

Prehistoric people must have noticed that this happened. So they began to mate certain kinds of wolves to get the kind of wolf they wanted. By mating only the very biggest and strongest wolves, most of the puppies would grow up to be big and strong, too. By keeping this up, people would soon have a whole group of wolves that were bigger and stronger than others. And of course, by mating small wolves, or by mating only long-nosed wolves, and so on, they slowly got wolves that looked quite different from the two they started with.

This is how different kinds, or breeds, of dogs began. And this is one reason why lap dogs such as the Pekingese, and hunting dogs such as the Dachshund, and many other breeds don't look a bit like their wolf ancestors. These dogs were changed, little by little, during many years, until people had just the kind of dog they wanted.

The big Siberian Husky looks much like a wolf. The little Pekingese looks nothing like a wolf. But wolves were probably the ancestors of both dogs.

Old breeds of dogs

People have been breeding different kinds of dogs
for thousands of years. Each kind of dog was
bred to do a certain kind of thing, whether it was
to hunt or just to look cute. But for a long, long
time, our prehistoric ancestors, whether they lived
in Europe, Africa, or Asia, lived by hunting. So
most of the first dogs, everywhere, were probably
bred to be hunters.

The way these dogs looked depended a lot on
where their ancestors had lived and how they
had gotten their food. In northern Europe, gray
wolves were probably the ancestors of dogs. These
large, sturdy wolves hunted big animals. And they
had heavy coats that kept them warm in the cold
climate. The dogs that came from these wolves
looked much like them.

Norwegian Elkhound

Not long ago, scientists in Norway found a cave containing the bones and tools of people who lived about seven thousand years ago. They also found the skeletons of two dogs. These dogs had been big, strong animals. They probably helped people hunt such creatures as deer, elk, and even bears, for food. Dogs very much like them are still with us today. They are the dogs we call Norwegian Elkhounds. This breed of dog is a tough, skillful hunter of big animals. And it looks much like a wolf.

Another dog of today that was bred long ago to hunt big animals is the Chow Chow. Chow Chows have lived in China for thousands of years, but an old Chinese legend says they were brought there by people called Tartars. The Tartars lived in a cold, northern desert outside China, and the Chow Chow still looks much like a shaggy, sturdy, northern wolf.

In a hot country such as Egypt, a very different kind of hunting dog was bred. The wolves there didn't need heavy fur; they were short-furred. They didn't hunt by sniffing out an animal's trail as the northern wolves did. These animals lived in broad, flat places where they could see for long distances. So they hunted by sight. They had keen eyes, long legs, and slim bodies.

Pictures and carvings made by Egyptian artists of four and five thousand years ago show us the kinds of hunting dogs the Egyptians bred. These dogs were slim, elegant-looking animals, with high, pointed ears and pointed noses.

Dogs much like them are still with us today. They are the dogs we call the Greyhound, the Saluki, the Ibizan Hound, the Pharaoh Hound, and the Afghan Hound. These are among the fastest of all dogs. Today, the Afghan Hound has a long coat. This probably came about because long ago its ancestors moved out of Egypt into the colder climate of Afghanistan.

Although the very first dogs were probably all hunters, there was soon a need for other kinds of dogs. About eleven thousand years ago, people learned how to grow plants and raise goats, sheep, and cattle for food. Now there was a new job for the dog—helping to guard its master's land and herds. So people began to breed guard dogs and herd dogs.

The skeleton of a prehistoric dog that probably served as a guard and helped care for a herd of animals was found in England some years ago. The dog lived about five thousand years ago, in a place where some prehistoric people had a farm.

Greyhound

Cardigan Welsh Corgi

Scientists can tell from the dog's teeth and bones that it was well-fed and well cared for. It was a big dog, of the kind we call a Mastiff, and could easily have fought off wolves. Bones of such Mastiff-type dogs have been found in other places, too, so we know these dogs were widely used for herding in prehistoric times.

But there was a need for little herd dogs, too. When the people called Celts moved into Wales about three thousand years ago, they brought with them the small, short-legged, pointy-eared Cardigan Welsh Corgi. At that time the Corgi was a valued hunter and watchdog. But, in time, the Celts became herdsmen. They then trained the Corgi to drive cattle out to pasture and bring them back. The little dogs would nip at the heels of the cattle and then crouch down to avoid the angry kick. After the pastures were fenced in, the Corgi almost disappeared. But because enough people loved these little dogs, they are still with us.

The Celts also settled in Ireland some three thousand years ago. And with them came the huge fierce-looking dogs with gentle hearts that are now called Irish Wolfhounds. The Wolfhound was used for hunting wolves and giant elk in Ireland for hundreds of years.

Long, long ago, people began to breed very small dogs that they wanted simply as pets and house dogs. The tiny, fluffy, long-haired dog that we call the Maltese was a favorite pet of the ancient Greeks some three thousand years ago. Many Greeks even built special tombs for these dogs. And the tiny Italian Greyhound, plainly a small version of the Greyhound, was bred by the Romans as a house dog.

Maltese

"New" breeds of dogs

Many breeds of dogs that are very popular today first appeared during the past thousand years. We might call these the "new" breeds of dogs, although many of these breeds have been around for hundreds of years. As with the "old" breeds, people had reasons for developing the newcomers.

About seven hundred years ago, the otters in the rivers and streams of Europe became a problem for fishermen. Otters eat fish, and the fishermen wanted the fish for themselves. They used dogs to hunt the otters, but these dogs were not good enough to suit the fishermen. So, dog breeders set about developing a dog that could really do the job.

In time, they had a big, strong dog with a heavy, waterproof coat and webbed feet—a dog that loved the water and could swim almost as well as an otter. Naturally, this new breed of dog was called an Otter Hound.

About four hundred years ago, the Germans developed the Great Dane. This dog's ancestry is lost in the mists of time, but it may be a cross between the Mastiff and the Irish Wolfhound. In

any event, the Germans got a giant dog that could hunt and fight. And this dog would have to do just that. It was bred to hunt wild boars, one of the most savage animals in Europe.

Why we call this dog a Great Dane is really something of a mystery. After all, the Great Dane comes from Germany, not Denmark. We took the name from the French, who at one time called this dog a *grand Danois,* or "Great Danish." The Germans call this dog *Deutsche dogge,* which loosely translates as "German mastiff." The Italians call it *alano,* a name that means "mastiff or boar hound." But by whatever name, the Great Dane is truly a great dog.

More than three hundred years ago, a Russian duke imported some fast Greyhound-type dogs to use for hunting. But these dogs had thin coats and couldn't take the bitterly cold Russian winters. So the duke crossed these dogs with a Russian dog that had a heavy coat like that of a Collie. The swift, hardy dogs that he got were the first Borzois, or Russian Wolfhounds.

Otter Hound

Dachshund

Dogs have long been used to hunt badgers. In Germany, this kind of dog was called a *dachshund.* The name comes from *dachs,* meaning "badger," and *hund,* meaning "dog." But it wasn't until about three hundred years ago that the breed we call the Dachshund first appeared in Germany.

You may think that, with their long bodies and short legs, these dogs look rather strange. And, compared to many dogs, they do look strange. But there's a reason. The Dachshund was bred to this shape so it could squeeze down a badger hole.

At first, there were only the Smooth and Longhaired types. Later, a Wirehaired type was bred. This type had a tough coat that protected it against sharp underbrush.

One of the youngest breeds is the Doberman Pinscher. These dogs come from Germany. They are named for Louis Dobermann, the man who was the original breeder. First bred as a guard dog and watchdog, the courageous Doberman has gained fame as a police dog and war dog.

Another more recent breed is the Chesapeake Bay Retriever. In the year 1807, an English ship was wrecked off the coast of Maryland. All those aboard, including two Newfoundland puppies, were saved. The grateful sailors gave both of the puppies, a male and a female, to their rescuers.

The new owners trained the dogs to retrieve ducks. Later, the two dogs were mated with other breeds of dogs, probably retrievers. In time, the breeders got a dog that could work for hours in the icy waters of Chesapeake Bay. Not surprisingly, they called this new breed of dog the Chesapeake Bay Retriever.

Still another new breed, one that goes back just about a hundred years, is the well-mannered Boston Terrier. This dog is a cross between an English Bulldog and a English Terrier.

At first, this "American gentleman among dogs" was called an American Bull Terrier. Breeders of Bull Terriers objected. So, because the dog was bred in Boston, it became known for all time as the Boston Terrier.

Chesapeake Bay Retriever

. . . .
Buy a pup and your money will buy
Love unflinching that cannot lie—
Perfect passion and worship fed
By a kick in the ribs or a pat on the head.
Nevertheless it is hardly fair
To risk your heart for a dog to tear.

. . . .
When the body that lived at your single will,
With its whimper of welcome, is stilled (how still!);
When the spirit that answered your every mood
Is gone—wherever it goes—for good,
You will discover how much you care,
And will give your heart to a dog to tear.

. . . .

from *The Power of the Dog*
Rudyard Kipling

4

Dogs to remember

Ajax

by Mary Elwyn Patchett

Australia is a land of contrasts. Sometimes the country suffers from a drought, and sometimes from rolling floods that carry away animals and houses, fences, and even people.

I remember only one such flood. While it was frightening and terrible, I could not help finding it exciting. And it did give me the most wonderful dog I have ever known—my golden giant, Ajax.

It had been raining for weeks, both at my home and far upriver. My father got news of the approaching flood by telephone, and so we had time to make preparations to leave and move to higher land.

When my father said we must get ready to move, I was very excited. We were to take tents and to go up to a hill about three miles from the homestead. There we would be above the water however much it should rise. First, everything possible had to be put away, so we helped stack furniture up in the big loft. Then the car was driven up a ramp onto a high veranda and chained there. It was no use to us. The water in the small gullies lying between us and the hill was already too deep to cross in the car.

We had to make our trek in buggies and sulkies and drays. Of course the station hands and their families were coming too. I was going in the sulky with Lewis, who was a wonderful bushman, full of the sort of stories that children love to listen to.

When we reached the hilltop, the men began setting up the tents. We had a campfire supper, and I was sent to bed almost as soon as it was dark. Algy, my Bulldog, and Ben, my Australian Terrier, lay on saddlecloths on the end of my camp stretcher. The whole place was wet and smelly. I was afraid of the rustling things that crawled about me in the dark, so I let Algy and Ben creep up on my bed and lie beside me, which in the ordinary way was strictly forbidden.

In the morning the water had fallen a few inches, and the dogs and I set out to explore.

I was running round a big log when I heard a whining, scratching sound in it. I listened and heard it again. So did the dogs. Benny began to dig violently at one end of the log. I pulled him away because I was afraid of what he might find in there. Then I marked the log, called the dogs and we raced back to the camp to find Lewis.

Lewis brought an ax and began to chop at the waterlogged bark. There was no sound from inside. I think Lewis thought that I had imagined the noise. Then a chip of wood came away, and underneath it we could see a bright, golden gleam. Lewis made the opening wider, put in his hand and pulled out a long, yellow puppy, quite dead.

"Well, there you are," Lewis said. "I'm afraid we are too late—the little chap's dead."

"Oh, Lewis, how awful! But how long has he been dead?"

"About a day—perhaps more, I should think."

"You mean he hasn't just died this minute?"

"No, he's quite cold. He's been dead some time."

"Then he can't be the one I heard!" I shouted excitedly. "There must be another one in there!"

Lewis began his careful chopping again. Sure enough another bright golden gleam appeared. He tore the soft wood away with his hands and my heart sank. There was no movement—apparently this little chap was as dead as his brother.

Lewis put his hand in to lift the pup and pulled it back, saying, "Ouch! He bit me, the little demon!"

"Oh, he's alive! He's alive!"

"He's alive all right, and he's got a mighty fine set of milk teeth."

Lewis put his hand back in the log much more cautiously. He lifted out another yellow pup, so nearly dead that it made little difference. But the pup still had enough spirit to draw back his tiny upper lip and snarl at the big man holding him.

Lewis handed him to me, saying, "Here you are. I don't think he'll live—he seems all in—so you mustn't be upset if you lose him. Take him back to camp and get some warm milk from your mother, and wrap him up warmly."

All that day I fed the pup on milk every hour. If he wasn't any stronger, he certainly hadn't lost strength. Then I fed him every two hours all through the night. My mother wanted to help me, but I wanted to care for him by myself.

The next morning the pup was brighter, and I was half dead with sleepiness!

By afternoon I was very sleepy. After I had fed the pup, I lay down beside him and went off to sleep. I must have slept very soundly, for when I woke the pup was not there. I jumped up and hurried to the tent flap, pushed it aside, and saw a sight I shall never forget.

Outside on the wet ground I saw a circle of dogs. In it were Algy and Ben and the sheep and cattle dogs belonging to the stockmen. In the center of the ring stood my tiny, savage, golden pup. He swayed on his legs, but a faint, ominous growl came from the small golden chest. His lips were drawn back, and his brilliant yellow eyes were filled with flickering pink lightnings. This wee, starved pup was defying a dozen full-grown dogs in his lonely, friendless world. My heart went out to him as I watched; his hind legs gave way and he sat down, but he still kept his head high and rumbled his tiny defiance of the crowd.

I couldn't bear it any longer, he was so alone. I stepped forward and picked him up. His sharp eyeteeth broke the skin on my hand and drops of blood welled out. I left my hand in his jaws, and he looked up at me uncertainly. I stroked his head with my other hand, and he opened his jaws. I kept on stroking him and presently he licked the salty blood off my hand, with a wondering expression in his eyes.

Then I held him against my face and whispered to him, "Do you know that you're *my* dog—that you're my Ajax, the bravest of the brave?"

He licked my cheek and that ended our first battle of wills. I had won—he was my dog, my Ajax, forever.

Once the flood began to go down, the river dropped rapidly. Actually I had had Ajax for only two days when my father decided that it would be safe to begin the trek home.

When we reached the homestead we found it in a horrible mess of mud and rubbish, but safe. Everyone worked at shoveling the mud out until hoses could be put on. Finally it was pretty clean, but it stayed damp and beastly for days.

Ajax grew into a tremendous dog. He never played with other dogs and he just tolerated humans. He seemed to get the exercise his huge

frame needed on long, nightly hunting trips from which he would return and throw himself down beside my bed until morning. I was the one thing he loved. He hardly took his deep yellow eyes off me. I hated to go anywhere without him. When I went away he was filled with savage despair.

In a couple of years he grew nearly as big as a calf, and his coat was a glorious orange-golden color. We decided his mother must have been a dingo—one of those clever, savage Australian wild dogs—and his father, most likely, was a big kangaroo dog. Kangaroo dogs are like giant greyhounds, very fast on their feet, with great deep chests and bony, intelligent heads.

When Ajax was three, my family took a house at the seaside for the summer. I was excited, but miserable at the thought of leaving the dogs behind, especially Ajax who would be so unhappy without me.

When we arrived at a quiet cove below Sydney called Half-Moon Bay, I was delighted. The bungalow overlooked the beach and the splendid, wild waters of the Pacific. The morning after we arrived, after spending nearly a week in Sydney on the way down, I was plunging about in the surf. A "dumper"—a big wave full of churning undertow—caught me, knocked me down, and landed me on the beach in a smother of sand and water. When I got my breath and opened my eyes, I was knocked down again—by Algy and Ben!

They scrabbled and yelped and smothered me. Algy, in moments of excitement, always imagined he was a tiny puppy again and wanted to sit on my knee. So there he was, knocking me down and trying to sit on me at the same time! When I managed to look up, Lewis was standing behind me, his dark face creased with laughter. I called out, "Oh, Lewis, how lovely—where's Ajax?"

"He's waiting in the garden. I didn't know how he'd take to the beach if there was a crowd here. I didn't realize it would be so quiet—"

"But how did you get here?"

"Well, I think you have to thank Ajax. I had an awful job with him after you left. He kept starting out to find you. So I wired to your father and got my orders to drive the truck down and bring all the boys along. We've covered about five hundred miles in the last four days. Look!"

He broke off and pointed to where, against the skyline on the edge of the sand, stood a colossal, orange-colored dog. The dog stood motionless for a second, and then I called "Ajax!" and he left the bank. He didn't seem to jump—he just launched himself into space. The next instant I was knocked flat and Ajax stood over me, his feet planted on each side of my body, his serious, savage eyes gazing into mine. The wild light died out of them, and I put my hand up to his muzzle.

He gave a little whine, strange from such a great, gaunt creature, and I think the only whine I ever heard him give. Then he put his head down and licked my face. I put my arms around his neck and pulled myself up. Then we all went home to breakfast.

Each of the dogs had a different approach to the surf. Benny rushed at it, biting the bubbles and wobbling ludicrously behind as he backed away from a wave. He always thought the waves were chasing him up the beach.

Algy mumbled in his chops, then put his head on one side until his expression said quite plainly, "Somebody's fooling me. I *won't* go in that great big bath!" Finally he licked at the froth, paddled a little where the sand was wet from the spent waves, decided that it was quite harmless after all and settled down to enjoy himself.

Ajax looked neither right nor left. He followed
me into a rushing wave, breasted it with me,
and calmly followed into deep water. He swam
beside me as if he had done it all his life. I
think Ajax really loved the water, apart from
his wish to stay near me. He was a very strong
swimmer and would tow me along whenever I put

my hand on his neck. Sometimes he let me swim
by myself, but he always lay on the sand and
watched until I came out again.

One fine morning I woke early and decided to
go for a swim. Ajax was off on one of his prowls
and I could hear Ben and Algy quarreling about
something at the back of the house. I decided to
trick them and slip off alone. It was high tide and
the sea looked oily and heavy, with no waves to
speak of. I decided that there was probably a
heavy undertow and that I must be careful. I
kicked off my sandals and waded in. The sudden,
crisp, cool shock of the water was wonderful, and
I began swimming.

Presently I thought I was far enough from the
shore and turned to swim in, but I couldn't. I
could feel the strong grip of the water drawing
me away from the beach. I knew I mustn't panic.
I let myself float to regain my strength, and was

alarmed to find that I was being carried seaward even more swiftly than I thought.

I was very afraid. I couldn't fight the undertow. And the sea was so deep and undisturbed it was likely to attract the deadly gray nurse sharks. It was a nasty thought. Those powerful, hungry fish might be cruising near me, quite unseen. I grew

more and more afraid. I tried to control myself, but as weariness crept over me terror mounted. I turned my head toward the shore and called despairingly, "Ajax! Ajax!"

It seemed minutes afterward, but it could only have been seconds, when I heard feet thudding on the beach. I turned my head. Bounding across the pale gold of the early-morning sands was the darker golden shape of Ajax.

He sprang from the hard-packed sand at the edge of the water like something launched from a catapult. I could see his great head moving strongly toward me across the terrifying waste of water. In a minute or so the head came nearer to me. As I put my arm across his neck, he turned toward the shore. I saw my father and Lewis there. They were struggling to launch the little boat we kept dragged up on the dry sand.

Even Ajax, strong swimmer though he was,

could make no headway against the terrible pull of the undertow. He could barely hold his own with my added weight dragging at him. I was too exhausted to help, and could only hang on and try not to hamper the dog too much. I thought I could hear my father shouting encouragement. But I felt even Ajax's great strength waning. His shoulders moved more slowly, though his gallant heart kept him trying.

I don't remember much more, although I became conscious that the boat was beside me. I had only one idea fixed firmly in my mind: I must not let go of Ajax. My father told me afterward that they just could not pry my hands loose from Ajax's neck. At one stage they decided to tow us in, but they, too, thought of the sharks. So, with a great struggle, they finally hauled the dog into the boat with me attached.

When we reached the beach my father rolled
me in his coat, made a sand pillow for my head
and told me to lie there quietly. For once in his
life Ajax lost his aloofness. No human face could
have expressed greater anxiety for a loved one.
He padded softly round me, every now and again
putting his head down close to mine, licking my
hand, and finally lying close beside me.

About the author   Mary Elwyn Patchett was born
in Australia. In the book *Ajax: Golden Dog of the
Australian Bush,* from which this story was taken,
she tells what it was like to grow up on an Australian
cattle station, or ranch. You may want to read some
of her other books, such as *Golden Wolf, Great
Barrier Reef,* or *Warrimoo.*

Budweiser

Fire is an animal's greatest enemy. Even the bravest, strongest, and biggest kinds of animals are terrified of flames. And a dog fears fire just as much as any other animal does. But one very courageous fourteen-month-old St. Bernard named Budweiser braved a roaring fire *three times* to rescue some little children!

Mr. and Mrs. B. M. Carter of John's Island, South Carolina, had their six young grandchildren visiting them. One night, just as Mrs. Carter was putting the children to bed, there were two sudden explosions. Part of the house burst into flames! Instantly, Budweiser rushed into the bedroom and seized the youngest child, a little four-year-old, by her shirt. Quickly, he dragged her out of the house.

Budweiser, a Saint Bernard, rescued these two little girls from a burning house.

The house was rapidly turning into a hot, fiery furnace, but without hesitation Budweiser raced back inside. This time he grabbed a five-year-old girl by the arm and pulled her out of the house. Meanwhile, Mrs. Carter brought all of the other children out safely.

Perhaps Budweiser thought there were still some children in the house. Or perhaps he was trying to rescue the Carters' other dog, a little Chihuahua named Tiny, who was Budweiser's special "pal." At any rate, the loyal St. Bernard headed back to the house a third time. But the whole building was now a mass of flames. The big dog could not make his way inside.

Except for Tiny, everyone got out of the house. The only one injured was Budweiser, who had burns on his paws. The brave St. Bernard was named America's Dog Hero for 1973. This award, presented by Ken-L Ration dog food, has been given to a brave dog each year since 1954.

Greyfriars' Bobby

More than a hundred years ago, the great city of Edinburgh in Scotland was a busy, bustling place. The narrow, bumpy streets were filled with horse-drawn carriages, carts, and wagons.

To this city every Wednesday morning, came a farmer named Mr. Grey. And at his side, trotting along on short legs that moved so fast they seemed to twinkle, was Bobby. Bobby was Mr. Grey's Skye Terrier—a small, intelligent, short-tailed kind of dog whose bright eyes and stubby legs were nearly covered by his long, flowing hair.

Mr. Grey would spend the morning at market. When the time-gun—a signal cannon that was fired at one o'clock—went off, Mr. Grey and Bobby would head for a small restaurant called Traill's Dining Rooms, which was not far from Greyfriars' Church. There, Mr. Grey and Bobby would have lunch. Lunch was always the same for the little dog—a crisp bun. Mr. Traill, who owned the restaurant, soon came to know the little dog well.

One Wednesday, the farmer and his dog did not appear at the restaurant. Several days passed. Then, one day as the time-gun sounded the hour of one o'clock, Mr. Traill was startled to see a small, thin, bedraggled-looking dog standing in his doorway. It was Bobby, and he was all alone.

"Why, I believe he's hungry," Mr. Traill said to himself. "He's come for a bun, same as always. But where is his master?" He took a bun and held it out to the dog. "Is that it, laddie? Are ye hungry?"

Bobby took the bun, and with the quick, happy sort of skip that a hungry dog often makes when given a bit of food, turned and trotted from the restaurant. Mr. Traill watched him go, wondering what had happened. Was the little dog lost? Had something happened to his master, the farmer Grey?

Next day, at the same hour, Bobby came to the

restaurant again. The kindly Mr. Traill quickly gave another bun to the hungry animal. Again, Bobby took it in his mouth and trotted off.

Overcome with curiosity, Mr. Traill followed him. With Traill close behind him, Bobby made his way to Greyfriars' churchyard. There, near a grave that looked to Mr. Traill as if it were new, the dog lay down and began to eat his bun.

With a lump rising in his throat, Mr. Traill walked over and peered down at the simple grave marker. It bore the name of old Grey—Bobby's master. Traill realized, now, why the dog looked so thin and uncared for. His master was dead, and little Bobby had been staying here, night and day, beside the grave. Only the terrible pangs of hunger had finally driven him to search for food. Perhaps the sound of the time-gun had reminded him of Traill's Dining Rooms and the buns he had gotten there.

Traill bent over the little dog. "Come away, laddie," he urged in a low, gentle voice. "It's no use—your master's gone. I'll take care of you." Bobby wagged his tail. But he did not budge. The man could not make him leave the grave. After a time, sadly shaking his head, Traill left.

Each day after that, always at the hour of one, Bobby came to beg for a bun, which Traill never failed to give him. The man told others about the faithful little Skye Terrier who would not leave his master's grave. Soon, most of the people in the city of Edinburgh knew of the dog.

Many people tried to coax Bobby away from the grave. But he refused to leave. Then some of Mr. Grey's relatives took the little dog away from the cemetery and tried to give him a home. But Bobby escaped, and returned to the grave! After a time, some of the citizens of Edinburgh raised money to have a shelter built beside the grave.

Now Bobby could take refuge from rain and snow, without leaving the graveside.

For fourteen years the little dog stayed beside his master's grave. He became so much a part of the cemetery that he was known as Greyfriars' Bobby. Visitors to the cemetery would see his small, gray form curled on the grass beside Grey's grave.

Then, one morning, someone noticed that Bobby lay in a stiff, unmoving position. The little Skye Terrier was dead.

Greyfriars' Bobby was buried next to Mr. Grey's grave. At last, the faithful dog, who had waited so long, was with his master again.

Bobby was a Skye Terrier who stayed by his master's grave for fourteen years. This statue of Bobby stands in the city of Edinburgh, Scotland.

Patches

It was a bitter cold December night. Mr. Marvin Scott, who lived by Lake Spanaway in the state of Washington, went down to the lake to check on a boat. With him was his dog, Patches, half Collie, half Malamute.

Suddenly, Mr. Scott slipped on the icy pier and fell, injuring both of his legs. Seconds later, he slid helplessly into the deep icy water! Unable to swim because of his injured legs, he sank below the surface. Suddenly he was grabbed by the hair. Patches had leaped into the water after him and was holding him tight!

When they came to the surface, Patches pulled his master to the dock, about twenty feet away. But when they reached the dock, Mr. Scott could not climb up. His legs were useless. The pain of his injuries, and the shock of the cold water, had made him faint. Once again, he sank into the

Patches, a brave mixed-breed saved his master's life three times in a single night.

water! And, once again, Patches came after him! Again, the dog seized his master and pulled him to the dock.

Mr. Scott came to. He realized that Patches, too, was in trouble. The dog, shivering with cold, was nearly exhausted. The man pushed Patches up onto the dock. Then, hanging on to the dock for dear life, he began to scream for help.

It was no use. No one could hear him. There was no one nearby and his house was too far away. But Patches seemed to understand what had to be done. The dog braced his feet. His jaws closed upon the collar of Mr. Scott's overcoat. Then Patches pulled and tugged, until Mr. Scott was able to pull himself up onto the dock. With Patches still tugging and pulling on his collar to help him, Mr. Scott was able to crawl to his house.

Patches, named America's Dog Hero for 1965, had saved his master's life—not once, but *three* times! A real dog to remember!

Barry

The towering, snow-covered Alps form a giant barrier between many of the countries of Europe. For thousands of years, the only way to get over these mountains was by means of passes. But there were many dangers.

When tired travelers lay down to rest, they often fell asleep. And in the dreadful cold high in the mountains, they could soon freeze to death. Or sudden blizzards might cause them to lose their way. Or huge masses of snow sliding down the mountainside might bury them.

Many hundreds of years ago, a man named Bernard de Menthon built a shelter in one of the passes between Switzerland and Italy. Monks who stayed at the shelter did what they could to help travelers. After a time, the monks began to use a special sort of dog to go out and search for travelers who were in trouble. By this time, the pass had become known as the Great St. Bernard Pass. So the dogs became known as St. Bernards.

The St. Bernards were trained to save lives. They could sniff out people from far away. They could even find people who were buried under the snow. They would cover freezing people with their bodies to warm them. And they would bark with their deep voices to show the monks of the shelter where to come.

The most famous of all these St. Bernards was named Barry. Barry lived about 150 years ago. This brave dog helped to save the lives of some forty people! He once saved a little boy who was trapped on an icy mountain ledge. The boy was asleep and freezing. Barry covered him with his big, warm body and licked his face to wake him. When the boy awoke, he climbed onto Barry's back. The great St. Bernard carried him to safety.

There is a story that Barry was killed by a
soldier who thought his rescuer was a wolf. But
Barry did not meet this sad end. He worked at
rescuing people for twelve years. Then the
monks sent him to the city of Bern, in Switzerland,
where he lived quietly for two more years. When
he died, his skin was stuffed and mounted. Barry
can still be seen in a museum in Bern.

To this day, the strongest and handsomest dog
in each litter born at the shelter is named Barry
—in honor of that brave Barry of long ago.

Taffy

Taffy, a Cocker Spaniel, helped to save her young master from drowning.

Taffy was a honey-colored Cocker Spaniel who belonged to Mr. and Mrs. Ken Wilson of Coeur d'Alene, Idaho. Her very special friend was the Wilson's three-year-old son, Stevie.

One day, Mr. Wilson took Stevie and Taffy with him when he went to look at a horse. The corral where the horse was kept was on the edge of a lake. Mr. Wilson put Stevie and Taffy in a safe place. Then he went to try out the horse.

A few minutes later, Taffy came racing up. She dashed around and around the horse, barking furiously. Then she charged away again, heading for the lake. Moments later she was back, her fur gleaming wetly. Desperately, she hurled herself at the horse, nipping at its legs and barking furiously.

Mr. Wilson suddenly realized that the dog was trying to tell him something. But what? *Stevie!* Something had happened to Stevie!

He threw himself from the horse's back and ran after Taffy, who was now speeding back to the lake. Fear stabbed through Mr. Wilson as he saw his son's red jacket floating in the water. Wading in, he found his son lying face down on the sandy bottom, in four feet of water!

Someone had let the boy and dog out of the safe place where Mr. Wilson had put them. Stevie had wandered to the lake and fallen in. But the boy was not dead, and he did not die. He was saved in the nick of time. Clever Taffy had been smart enough to make Mr. Wilson understand that something was wrong, and then lead him to the place where he was needed! Taffy was selected as America's Dog Hero for 1955.

A race against death

The tiny cabin was one of a few small buildings that looked like dark dots against the snow. Two men peered through the cabin window at the swirling blizzard raging outside. The fury of the wind made the walls rattle.

"Twenty-eight below zero," muttered one of the men. "And that wind's blowin' stronger than ever! She ain't going to let up any."

The other man, a tall, husky giant, nodded. "What time is it, Charlie?"

Charlie pulled out a battered pocket watch and looked at it. "'Bout a quarter to ten."

The big man turned abruptly away from the window. "Well, I'm going to start, Charlie. No sense in waiting any longer. This blizzard could blow for days." He picked up a sealskin parka and slipped it over his head. It was followed with a second parka made of thick cloth. "Help me hitch up the team."

The two men stepped out of the cabin into the storm-blown night. A big, black dog with one white foreleg came with them. Outside stood a large, rather flimsy-looking wooden sled. And clustered about the sled, lying and sitting in the snow, were twelve more large, shaggy dogs.

Working swiftly, the two men tied the dogs in pairs, forming a "chain" that was hitched to the front of the sled. The big, black dog that had followed them from the cabin was tied by itself at the head of the team. The tall man knelt down beside this dog and stroked its head.

Balto was the lead dog on one of the dog teams that brought medicine to Nome, Alaska, when a diphtheria epidemic struck that city in 1925.

"We've got a tough run to make, Balto," he murmured. "But we can do it, eh boy?"

The big dog looked up at him with bright, intelligent eyes. Balto was the leader of the dog team, picked because he was the smartest and most experienced of all the dogs.

Charlie had stepped back into the cabin. Now he came out again, carrying a large package wrapped in furs. "Here's the stuff, Gunnar."

Gunnar Kaasen took the package and tied it carefully in the sled. Because of what was in this package he was about to risk his life and the lives of all his dogs. He and his team of dogs were going to carry the package some thirty-five miles to the little town of Safety. The journey would take about five hours, through bitter cold and clawing wind. At Safety, another dog team would pick up the package and carry it on to the city of Nome. Already, nineteen teams, working in relays, had traveled more than six hundred miles with the package.

The package meant *life* for hundreds of people. An epidemic had struck the city of Nome, Alaska. The hideous, choking disease called diphtheria was raging in the city. Scores of people had been stricken. Some were already dead. More would die unless the package reached Nome quickly. And, unless the disease were checked, it would spread through the territory, killing thousands!

Only dog teams could get through to Nome. No trains ran in this part of Alaska in 1925. And the airplanes of that time were grounded by the cold. Even if they had been able to get into the air, they could not have flown in such a storm.

So Gunnar Kaasen knew he could not wait for the blizzard to pass. He had to leave now, at once. The package in his sled contained serum with which people could be given shots that would save them from the dreadful disease. He was in a race against death!

Kaasen stepped onto the sled runners that stuck out at the rear. With his gloved hands he gripped the two handles that curved up from the sled's high back. "So long, Charlie," he called. Then, raising his voice against the howl of the wind, he roared, "Mush!"

Mush! It was the signal to the lead dog that meant "go!" And Balto, trained to move the instant he heard that word, leaped forward. The other dogs immediately followed their leader. The sled slithered forward, quickly picking up speed as it began to slide smoothly over the snow.

The tiny town of Bluff, from which Kaasen had just set out, was at the edge of the sea. Kaasen guided the sled along the shore. He felt that he would make better time along the flat, open shoreland than he would inland.

The cold wind clawed at him. He could feel its sharpness even through his sealskin parka and pants. The rushing torrent of icy snowflakes stung his cheeks like needles and the moisture of his breath froze in the below-zero cold.

Minutes passed and lengthened into an hour or more. Kaasen was conscious only of the numbing cold and the wind. Because of the swirling snow, he could not see much beyond Balto running at the head of the team. But he knew this trail. He had traveled it many times before. Each familiar landmark that the team passed was just like a signpost guiding the way.

They were making good time, and had already reached the Topkok River. The sled's runners hissed over the ice-covered river.

Suddenly Balto stopped. At once the other dogs halted, too. Kaasen hurried forward to see what had happened. To his dismay, he saw that Balto had run into an overflow—a place where water had come up through the ice and had not yet frozen. Balto's paws were wet, and that could mean trouble. His wet feet would stick to the ice as he ran, and would soon be torn and bleeding.

Quickly, Kaasen guided the team into a nearby snowdrift. He spent precious minutes carefully drying off Balto's paws.

As soon as the dog was tended to, the man started the team running again. Crossing the river, they started up the side of the great hill that loomed above it. And at the top of Topkok hill, Kaasen ran into the full fury of the storm!

Icy snowflakes rushed through the air in a blinding cloud, pushed by the tremendous force of the howling, battering, eighty-mile-an-hour wind! The biting, burning cold held Kaasen in a grip that might have frozen the sun.

Desperately, Kaasen squinted ahead into the white-filled darkness. He could no longer even see the wheel dog, the one nearest the sled. It was as if he were alone, floating in the center of a frozen, white cloud. He couldn't tell whether he was still on the trail or not. He couldn't even guess where he was.

Kaasen was faced with a terrible problem. He could no longer guide the team. But he could not stop, and he could not turn back. He could only go on, hoping the dogs could stay on the trail.

"Balto," he muttered to himself. "It's up to you, Balto. You've got to get us there!"

At the front of the team, the big black husky ran steadily over the snow. His jaws were open and his red tongue lolled out of his mouth as he panted with the effort of his run. Perhaps he sensed that his master was no longer guiding the team. But it did not matter. Although as blinded by the blowing snow as the man, Balto did not have to rely on his eyes. He had his nose, his marvelous sense of smell, to keep him on the trail.

Hundreds of dog teams had followed this trail in the past, and Balto could sniff out the scent they had left, even through the packed snow. He was simply following a trail of scent. Now he was truly the leader of the team, leading even his master, who was helpless in the fierce blizzard.

The team sped down the long slope of the hill, across six miles of flat plain, and over ice-covered Spruce Creek. The dogs had now covered about thirteen miles. Somewhere ahead was the tiny town of Solomon, which lay on the coast, about thirty-three miles from Nome. There was a message for Kaasen in Solomon, a message telling him to wait until the blizzard was over, telling him that no man or dog could possibly face the terrible fury of the storm.

But Kaasen was not even aware that his team was anywhere near Solomon. He could hardly see his hands on the handles of the sled. And Balto did not know that he should stop at this place. The dog would simply run until his master told him to stop—or until he could run no more. So, in the snow-filled darkness, Kaasen's team raced on past the town.

Now they hit a long stretch of very high, open country. The wind was so fierce that it rocked the sled. More than once the sled tipped over in the loose snow. When this happened, Kaasen would have to make his way down the line of dogs and, working mainly by feel, untangle the harness.

On the team went, led by Balto. Then the trail turned, and the team had the wind at its back. At last they came to the little town of Safety. This was where Kaasen was supposed to turn the package of serum over to the driver of another team. This driver would take it on to Nome. But the cabin was dark. Kaasen was not expected before daylight, so everyone had gone to bed.

Kaasen decided not to stop. He did not want to waste precious time waiting for the other driver to dress and hitch up his team. Nome was only

some twenty-one miles away. Kaasen felt that his team could make it. They *would* make it!

At 5:30 in the morning Kaasen's team reached the snow-covered streets of Nome. In seven and a half hours they had covered fifty-three miles in the worst kind of weather. The sled dogs were panting and exhausted. Two of them were half frozen and limping badly. One side of Kaasen's face was frozen. But they had won—they had won the race against death!

After delivering the package of serum, Kaasen staggered up the line of dogs. He fell to his knees beside Balto. Crying softly, he wrapped his arms around the big dog's neck. "Balto," he sobbed. "Damn fine dog! You brought us through!"

Ten months later, Balto, Gunnar Kaasen, and a crowd of several hundred people stood in Central

Park in New York City. Many people in New York had raised the money to have a statue made and placed in the park. And now the statue was finished. Today, with speeches and tribute, it would be shown for the first time.

It was a bronze statue of Balto. But this statue was to honor all of the more than 150 dogs that had helped win the race to Nome.

The statue of Balto, his name carved in the rock, still stands in Central Park. Beneath the statue is a bronze plaque that bears these words:

A statue of Balto stands in Central Park in the city of New York.

DEDICATED TO THE INDOMITABLE SPIRIT OF
THE SLED DOGS
THAT RELAYED ANTITOXIN SIX HUNDRED MILES OVER ROUGH ICE
ACROSS TREACHEROUS WATERS THROUGH ARCTIC BLIZZARDS FROM
NENANA TO THE RELIEF OF STRICKEN NOME IN THE
WINTER OF 1925
ENDURANCE   FIDELITY   INTELLIGENCE

Grizzly Bear

The pet of Mr. and Mrs. Gratias of Denali, Alaska, was a big, gentle St. Bernard. The dog's full name was a tongue twister—Polar Blu Samaritan von Barri! But because the animal was so husky and bearlike, everyone called him "Grizzly Bear."

One spring day Mrs. Gratias heard a noise in her backyard. With Grizzly Bear at her side, she went to see what was going on. There, nosing about in the yard, was a small grizzly bear cub. Mrs. Gratias knew that the cub's mother must be nearby. And a mother grizzly bear with cubs is a very dangerous animal! The woman turned to hurry back into the house. But, suddenly, there was the mother bear!

Mrs. Gratias tried to get away, but she slipped on the icy ground and fell flat on her back. At once, the huge beast was upon her. One great claw ripped her cheek, the other tore into her shoulder. The bear lowered its head to sink its teeth into her throat.

At that moment, the dog, Grizzly Bear, went into action. The giant bear was three times his size, but that did not stop him. He hurled himself against the bear, making it stagger back. Then the St. Bernard, his eyes blazing and his teeth bared, put himself between Mrs. Gratias and the bear, ready to defend his mistress with his life!

Mrs. Gratias does not know what happened then. She fainted from loss of blood. When she came to, Grizzly Bear was anxiously licking her face. Of the real grizzly bear, there was no sign. The brave, loyal St. Bernard, named America's Dog Hero for 1970, had driven it off!

Grizzly Bear, a brave Saint Bernard, saved his mistress from a real grizzly bear.

Bingo is kind and friendly,
  A gentleman right to the core,
But he can't bear rats
And he hates all cats
  And the fuzzy brown dog next door.

There's a nice little girl who lives there,
  But they glare at us more and more;
So we never can call,
And the cause of it all
  Is the fuzzy brown dog next door.

Bingo is limping a little
  And one of his ears is sore,
He's rather a fright,
But, oh, what a sight
  Is the fuzzy brown dog next door!

Bingo Has an Enemy
Rose Fyleman

5

Dogs all around us

Ribsy and the apartment house

by Beverly Cleary

Henry Huggins' dog Ribsy was a plain ordinary city dog, the kind of dog that strangers usually called Mutt or Pooch. They always called him this in a friendly way, because Ribsy was a friendly dog. People liked Ribsy, and Ribsy liked people. But today Ribsy was alone and lost.

Ever since Ribsy had jumped out of the family car, he had been wandering around the strange neighborhood. The sidewalk gave him the scent of many people, dogs, and cats. But it did not give him the scent of his master, Henry Huggins.

There was little grass in this neighborhood and not many bushes, although there were a number of fire hydrants. Many of the buildings came right to the sidewalk, and most of them were of brick and were three or four stories high.

It was in front of one of these buildings that Ribsy first saw the boy with the tennis ball. Naturally Ribsy was interested in a boy with a tennis ball.

While Ribsy was watching the boy, a young woman came out of the apartment house. She was wearing a black coat over the starched dress and apron of a waitress. "Now see here, Larry Biggerstaff," she said, "you keep out of trouble today. I don't want to hear any more complaints from the manager about you."

Larry heaved a big sigh to show that he was disgusted with the whole situation. "But Mom, there's nothing to *do*."

"At noon you come to the café and get your lunch. In the meantime, keep out of trouble."

Larry began to bounce the tennis ball, which

was old and had lost much of its life. Ribsy
pranced up and wagged his tail to show that he
was ready to play.

Larry did not understand. "Go away, you old
dog," he said crossly. Ribsy barked to tell him
that here was a dog ready to play with a tennis
ball. Larry backed away. He dropped the ball,
and Ribsy picked it up.

"You gimme back my ball," said Larry. Ribsy
dropped the ball and stood over it, wagging his
tail.

Cautiously Larry advanced toward the ball, but
when he was about to pick it up, Ribsy grabbed
it in his jaws and went racing up the street.

"Hey!" yelled Larry.

Ribsy raced back, dropped the ball at Larry's
feet, and stood waving his tail and looking
hopefully up at the boy.

"Well thanks, pal," said Larry, surprised and
pleased.

"Wuf!" answered Ribsy.

The boy finally understood. He threw the ball

down the street, and Ribsy bounded after it, darting between the people who were walking along the sidewalk, and catching it on the first bounce. He was delighted and so was Larry. The boy threw the ball again and again for Ribsy to retrieve. Finally, Larry sat down on the front steps of the apartment house, and Ribsy threw himself down at his feet to pant.

"You're a pretty nice dog," remarked Larry. "You hungry?"

Ribsy thumped his tail on the sidewalk.

"You wait here," said Larry. "No, that wouldn't work. You might run off while I was getting you something to eat. Can you be real quiet?"

Again Ribsy thumped his tail.

"Come on then. I'll get you some cornflakes or a wienie or something," said Larry, and pulled a key out of his pocket. Ribsy followed him up the stairs, and Larry unlocked the front door. He tiptoed past the door of the apartment occupied by the manager of the building to an old-fashioned elevator. Ribsy was ready to enjoy this new game the boy was playing. Larry opened a glass door and folded back a metal gate, and Ribsy followed him into what appeared to be a small square room without windows. Larry closed the gate and the door, and pushed a button on the wall.

There was a whirring noise. Suddenly Ribsy had a feeling he had never felt before. He felt as if he was going up while his stomach stayed down. He did not like the feeling one bit. He did not like this strange little room. He wanted out right now. He began to bark.

"Sh-h-h!" Larry seemed upset by something. He scowled and grabbed at Ribsy. "Sh-h-h! She'll hear you."

The manager had already heard. A door on the first floor flew open, and a woman's cross voice called up, "Larry Biggerstaff. You get that dog out of this building at once!"

By that time the little room had stopped at the second floor. Larry slid back the gate and opened the glass door. Before stepping out, he whispered, "You stay right here. I'll come back and get you in a minute." Then he left the frightened dog and shut him in the little room.

Ribsy did not want to stay in the little room, but there was no way he could get out. Suddenly he felt himself beginning to rise again while his stomach seemed to stay behind. He barked for Larry to come and get him out of this place, but all he heard was the whir of machinery and the thump of Larry's sneakers running downstairs.

As the elevator stopped on the third floor and his stomach caught up, Ribsy heard Larry's frightened voice coming up the elevator shaft from the first floor. "Dog? What dog?" he was saying. "I don't have any dog."

"Don't you lie to me," the manager said. "I know there's a dog in this building."

"It isn't my dog," said Larry.

Upstairs a woman opened the door and pushed back the gate.

"Hello," said the woman to Ribsy, as if she met dogs in elevators every day. "How did you manage to press the button?"

This time Ribsy was taking no chance of being left in this frightening room that made him lose his stomach. He dashed past the woman and into the third-floor hall. Now he did not know what to do. He was in a long hall with doors on either side. At one side of the hall was a staircase, and at the end of the hall was a window with a fire-escape sign over it.

Larry's voice came up the stairwell. "But I don't *have* a dog."

"Young man," said Mrs. Kreech, "you took a dog into that elevator. You can't fool me."

Ribsy heard the elevator door open down on the first floor and the manager say in quite a different voice, "Oh, good morning, Mrs. Berg. I was looking for a dog in the elevator."

"There's no dog in the elevator," said Mrs. Berg, who was a friend of Larry's.

Ribsy stood listening at the steps, but all he heard was the elevator door close and the machinery whir. As the elevator rose, Ribsy started cautiously down the steps. He did not know what to expect in this strange building where rooms went up in the air. The second floor looked exactly like the third.

Larry's worried face appeared. "I've got to get you out of here," he whispered. "Come on." He started to lead Ribsy on down the steps, when the door of the manager's apartment opened on the first floor.

"We can't go down that way," whispered Larry. "Come on, this way." Larry led Ribsy down the hall toward the back stairs, which were near the window with the sign over it. He was about to start down with Ribsy when he heard someone coming up.

"I don't know who it is, but I'm not taking any chances," Larry muttered, looking around wildly. He saw the window at the end of the hall and opened it.

Ribsy found himself being picked up, thrust through the window, and dropped onto the fire escape. The window was closed behind him and a curtain pulled. Ribsy's feet slid through the metal bars of the fire escape and stuck down in empty space. If an elevator was a strange place, a fire escape was much, much worse. Ribsy felt as if he should be falling but, instead, there he hung in midair. He struggled to get all four of his feet up onto the metal bars of the fire escape.

Ribsy had to move his feet carefully on the cold metal or they would slip through. It made him uneasy to see the ground so far below. There was an opening in the fire escape big enough to jump through, but the ground was too far down.

Since Ribsy could not go down, he did the next best thing. He went up. He climbed up cautiously, one step at a time. Unfortunately, when he reached the next level of the fire escape, things were worse. The good solid ground was farther away. Ribsy peered into the window, but the third-floor hall was empty.

Bewildered and frightened, Ribsy lay down on the fire escape as best he could. He felt more lost than he had ever felt before. A half hour went by and then an hour. Larry did not come back.

Ribsy got up and managed to shake himself without having his feet slip through the fire escape. Cautiously he walked around the fire escape to make sure he had not missed a way out. There were only the ladderlike steps, and while he had not minded climbing up, they were much too steep to go down.

Ribsy became frantic. He felt as if the whole world had gone off and left him. He barked and barked and barked. There must be somebody who would come and get him off this thing.

And there was somebody. Somebody way down below on the next street. "Ribsy!" It was Henry Huggins' voice coming from the station wagon moving along with the rest of the traffic. Henry had his head out of the window and was pointing up at the fire escape.

At the sound of the voice he loved, Ribsy went wild. He barked until he was hoarse. In his excitement his hind feet slipped through the fire escape. Terrified lest he should fall through, he scrambled frantically to regain his footing on the metal bars. When his feet were planted safely once more, there was no sign of Henry anyplace.

Suddenly Ribsy saw Henry Huggins appear from around the side of the building. "Ribsy!" the boy shouted. "I've found you!"

Next Ribsy saw Henry's mother and father come around the corner. "I finally found a parking space," remarked Mr. Huggins, and looked up at Ribsy. "Hello there, fellow."

"See, Dad," said Henry. "I told you if we just drove around in this neighborhood we were sure to find him."

"You were right, Henry," said his mother. "But how on earth do you suppose he got up there?"

"What worries me is how we are going to get him down," said Henry.

"That's easy," Mr. Huggins was saying. "I'll just go ring the bell and tell the manager we want our dog back."

By this time Larry Biggerstaff had arrived. "Please don't do that," begged Larry, bursting into the conversation. "The dog isn't supposed to be there. I'll catch it if the manager finds out about him. I shoved him out on the fire escape to hide him. And, well, I have been sitting out on the front steps trying to figure out how I was going to get rid of him without the manager seeing me."

"We seem to have a problem," remarked Mr. Huggins, looking up at the dog on the fire escape.

Ribsy could not be patient any longer. He put his paw on the top step. Then he reached for the second step and at the same time brought his hind feet down to the top step. It was too late to turn back. He found himself coming down the steps faster than he expected. Halfway down he slipped and tumbled, yelping, to the bottom, and there he was with his feet dangling in space again.

Ribsy picked himself up and scrambled around trying to find places to set his feet.

"Did you hurt yourself, Ribsy?" Henry asked.

Ribsy managed to set his feet on the slats of the fire escape. "Wuf!" he said, and wagged his tail to show that he was still all right.

Two men from the body-and-fender shop next door came out to see what all the commotion was about. "There's a ladder in the shop that should reach almost to the bottom of the fire escape," one of them said. "I'll get it." He returned in a moment with a paint-spattered stepladder, which he set up under the fire escape. It almost reached the metal ladder that extended down from the fire escape.

Mr. Huggins climbed the stepladder and then the short ladder that was part of the fire escape. He crawled through the opening in the lower level of the fire escape and picked up Ribsy. "Hold still, boy," he said, as Ribsy gratefully tried to lick his face.

"You'll fall," worried Mrs. Huggins. "You can't possibly climb down the fire-escape ladder and the stepladder with a dog."

"Don't drop him," begged Henry.

"I'm afraid that's what I will have to do," said Mr. Huggins.

"Go ahead," said one of the body-and-fender men. "We'll catch him."

Ribsy felt himself being lifted over the railing of the fire escape, and then he experienced a terrible moment of panic as he fell through the air. Suddenly everything was all right. Four strong hands caught him. Ribsy wriggled out of the grasp of the body-and-fender men and sprang into Henry's arms.

"Ribsy!" said Henry. "Ribsy, old boy!" He sank to his knees and hugged his dog.

"And now I think we'd better go home before Larry's manager catches us," said Mr. Huggins, as the men took down the ladder and carried it into the body-and-fender shop.

Henry, his parents, and Larry walked along the side of the apartment house with Ribsy bounding along beside them. In front of the building they ran right into Mrs. Kreech, who was sweeping the front steps.

"I knew you had a dog, Larry Biggerstaff," she said triumphantly. "Wait till I talk to your mother about this!"

"There must be some mistake," said Mr. Huggins politely. "This is our dog. He never belonged to Larry."

"But—" began Mrs. Kreech.

"No," said Mr. Huggins firmly. "The dog is ours, and has been for several years. We just— misplaced him for a while."

About the author Beverly Cleary's interest in writing began in the sixth grade. She says, "I do not think about writing for children. I write the stories I enjoy telling. I am fortunate that children enjoy reading them." If you liked this story, you'll like *Ribsy*, the book from which it was taken.

Dog tales

People have been putting dogs into stories and books for thousands of years. In fact, there is a dog in a story that was written in Greece nearly three thousand years ago.

This story, called the *Odyssey,* tells about the many adventures of a king named Odysseus, or Ulysses. When Odysseus finally reaches his home after nearly twenty years, only his old hunting dog Argos recognizes him. The old dog's ears move and he wags his tail. But he is too old and weak to get up. Then, happy that he has lived to see his beloved master once more, Argos dies.

Since that time, dogs have appeared in many other stories. Whole books have been written about the adventures of dogs. And many of these books have been made into motion pictures.

The famous book, *Lassie Come-Home,* by Eric Knight, is the story of the struggles of a Collie to find the master from whom she has been separated. Another famous dog story is *The Call of the Wild,* by Jack London. This book tells of the adventures of Buck, who becomes first a sled dog and then the leader of a wolf pack in Alaska during the gold rush days. *Silver Chief, Dog of the North,* by Jack O'Brien, and *Wilderness Champion,* by Joseph Lippincott, are two other tales of dogs in the far north.

The book *The Hundred and One Dalmatians,* by Dodie Smith, is a funny story about a number of dogs and other animals that work together to save some puppies from a cruel woman who wants to make a fur coat of them. *Star Dog,* by A. M. Lightner, is about a dog that can talk to his master and is as smart as a human. And *Sounder,* by William Armstrong, is about a poor black family in the South and their Coonhound, Sounder.

*Dogs are the heroes or main
characters in many fine books.*

Each section of this book begins with a dog
story. Most of the stories were taken from books
about dogs. At the end of many of these stories,
you will find the titles of other dog books. And
on pages 293–294, there are still more titles of
dog books that you may want to read.

Dogs in art

People have liked dogs for thousands of years. So it isn't surprising that artists in all parts of the world have put dogs into works of art since the earliest of times.

The very oldest paintings with dogs in them were made by prehistoric artists as much as ten thousand years ago. These pictures show men and their dogs out hunting.

In ancient Egypt, four thousand years ago, artists made many bright, exciting paintings of

This wooden statue of Anubis, an Egyptian god of the dead, was carved more than three thousand years ago. Found in the tomb of a Pharaoh, this ancient Anubis looks like today's Ibizan Hound.

A prehistoric artist painted this picture of a hunter and his dog thousands of years ago. The painting can still be seen on the side of a cliff in Algeria.

Egyptian kings using dogs to hunt lions and other beasts. The Egyptian artists also made wooden carvings of dogs that look much like the greyhounds of today.

More than three thousand years ago, there was a city called Ur in the country we now know as Iraq. The artists of Ur made lifelike clay models of dogs. One artist made a vase in the shape of a Mastiff lying down.

There are pictures of dogs on many ancient Greek vases. One vase shows two dogs fighting. Another shows two men feasting—and under the table a dog is enjoying its bit of the feast!

In Rome, two thousand or more years ago, wealthy people often had large pictures called murals painted on the walls of their houses. There were dogs in many of these paintings.

This Grecian vase, made about 2,600 years ago, shows a vase seller trying to stop two dogs that are fighting and knocking over his vases.

Mosaics are pictures made of colored stones. In the Roman mosaic, above, made about 1,600 years ago, a man and dog are hunting a wild boar. Below, a Roman mosaic, about 2,200 years old, says "Beware of the dog."

This four-hundred-year-old picture of a French king and his court also shows a pet Italian Greyhound.

An Indian in the land we now call Mexico made this statue of a fat little dog about 1,700 years ago.

The famous French artist Renoir painted this family portrait about a hundred years ago. The dog one of the children is sitting on was a Newfoundland named Porto.

In Europe, during the Middle Ages, dogs and hunters were a favorite subject for painters and tapestry weavers. Later, when artists were painting pictures of wealthy people, pet dogs were often a part of the picture.

Today, most of the pictures we see of dogs are photographs. But some artists are showing dogs in different ways—with statues made of welded metal or of wire. It's even possible to use a computer to make a picture of a dog!

147

Dog memorials

In many parts of the world people have put up statues and memorials in honor of dogs.

Some memorials honor certain kinds of dogs for their work. On the shore of Lake Tekapo, in New Zealand, there is a statue of a Collie. This memorial honors all of the sheep dogs without whose help the grazing of sheep in that mountain country would be impossible. And on the wall of a post office in Toronto, Canada, there is a stone carving in honor of the sled dogs that at one time were used to deliver mail.

There are also memorials in honor of individual dogs. In Tokyo, Japan, there is a statue of a dog named Hachiko. Hachiko was the kind of dog called an Akita, after a Japanese city. Hachiko belonged to Dr. Eisaburo Ueno, a professor at Tokyo University. Each morning, the dog would walk with his master to the train station. And each evening he would be waiting at the station to greet the professor and walk home with him.

But one evening the professor was not on the train. He had died that day, while working at the university. Hachiko waited patiently until nearly midnight, then went home by himself.

For the next nine years, the faithful dog went to the station every afternoon to wait for his master. When Hachiko died, people of Japan and several other countries collected money to have a statue of him put up in the railroad station.

Near the town of Gundagai, in Australia, there is a statue of a dog sitting on a box. The statue represents a dog in a poem. The poem tells of a dog that was set to guard his master's tucker

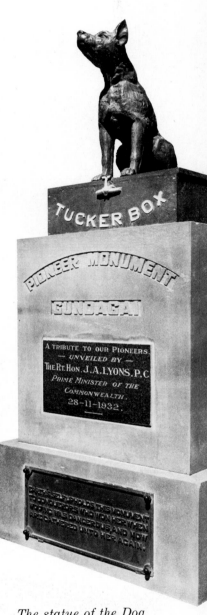

The statue of the Dog on the Tucker Box is famous in Australia.

A bronze statue in New Zealand honors all the sheep dogs of that country.

This statue of Old Drum,
a Coonhound, stands in
Warrensburg, Missouri.

A TRIBUTE TO THE DOG
(BY SENATOR GEORGE GRAHAM VEST)

A stone carving on a post office wall in Toronto, Canada, honors the sled dogs that once helped deliver Canadian mail.

box, or food box, while the master went away. The master never came back. But, until it died, the faithful dog continued to guard the box.

In Warrensburg, Missouri, in the United States, there is a statue of another real dog, a Black and Tan Coonhound called Old Drum. Old Drum, a hunting dog, didn't really do anything special. He became famous because of a speech made about him by George Vest, a United States Senator. The Senator spoke about the friendship and faithfulness of all dogs. Many years later, a statue of Old Drum, and a plaque with part of the speech on it, were put up at the place where the speech was made. Although the statue is of Old Drum, it really honors all dogs.

This statue of Hachiko, a famous Akita, is in Tokyo, Japan.

The proverbial dog

In every part of the world, people have wise old sayings that give good advice. Such sayings are called proverbs. In many proverbs, dogs, and their habits, are used to make a point.

Did anyone ever tell you to "Let sleeping dogs lie"? This is just another way of saying, "Let well enough alone," or, "Don't mess around with something that's all right as it is." This saying probably comes from the idea that if you wake a sleeping dog it might be startled and bite you.

A very old saying is, "If you lie down with dogs, you'll get up with fleas." This means that if you spend a lot of time with people who have bad habits or bad ways, you'll soon have some of their bad habits and bad ways.

People often say, "You can't teach an old dog new tricks." This means that it's hard to get someone to change old habits.

There is an old Danish proverb that says, "A dog's kennel is no place to keep a sausage." This means that you shouldn't put something you want in a place where someone else might be tempted to take it for themselves.

Have you ever heard someone say, "Barking dogs never bite," or "Every dog has his day," or "If you want a dog to follow you, feed him"? Can you guess what these proverbs mean?

Dog talk

Have you ever read a book that had "dog-eared" pages? Did someone ever "dog your footsteps"? Were you ever "sick as a dog"? Dogs are so much a part of our lives that our language is filled with expressions like these.

A "dog-eared" page is one that has a corner folded over, so that it looks like the floppy ear of a dog. And when you "dog" someone's footsteps, you follow close behind them, just as a dog follows the person it loves. And when you are "sick as a dog," you are *very* sick.

You might hear someone say that he or she "leads a dog's life." This means that the person has a rather miserable life, with much bad luck and unhappiness. And you might hear a friend say that he did something his teacher didn't like, so he is "in the doghouse." Your friend means that he feels like a dog hiding in its doghouse for fear of being punished.

People will sometimes say that a building, or a town, or a park is "going to the dogs." This just means that the place is getting old and dingy and is in need of repairs. If you hear someone say that something is "a real dog," they mean that the thing is no good. When people dress up and act fancy, it's often said that they are "putting on the dog."

When two dogs fight, they often circle around one another for some time before one of them pounces. In a war, enemy airplanes circle and dive at one another in much the same way. And so, an air battle is called a "dogfight."

hunting dog on Argentine bill

An Elkhound (above) is shown on a Norwegian coin and a Greyhound (below) appears on an Irish coin.

Dogs, dogs, everywhere!

If you look around you, you'll see pictures of dogs almost everywhere. Many countries have pictures of dogs on stamps, on paper money, and on coins. Pictures of dogs often appear in newspaper and magazine ads. Try to identify the breeds shown in the ads. Do the breeds seem to go with the things that are advertised?

A bus company that is named after a dog—the Greyhound—has a running Greyhound painted on all of its buses. And a company that makes records uses as its symbol a picture of a dog listening to a record.

There's even a "dog" in the sky! People of long ago thought that one group of stars seemed to have the shape of a dog. They named this group of stars, or constellation, the Big Dog. One of the stars in the group is called Sirius, or the Dog Star. It is the brightest star in the sky.

154

mongrel on U.S. stamp

Vizsla on Hungarian stamp

Great Dane on Bulgarian stamp

Akita on Japanese stamp

Polish Hound on Polish stamp

Cartoon and comic-strip dogs

Who doesn't know who Pluto is? Why, of course, he's Mickey Mouse's long-tailed, floppy-eared dog who's always getting into all kinds of trouble! And who doesn't know Snoopy, Charlie Brown's clever dog in the comic-strip "Peanuts"?

There are many comic strips and cartoons that feature dogs, or are all about a dog's adventures. And most of these comic-strip and cartoon dogs are better known than many famous real people! You'll probably recognize most of the cartoon and comic-strip dogs shown here.

Rivets   *George Sixta*

Tramp, a homeless, freedom-loving mutt, and Lady, a purebred dog who belongs to a family, enjoy a meal at a restaurant in the full-length Walt Disney cartoon, "Lady and the Tramp."

Little puppy with the black spots,
Come and herd the flock with me.
We will climb the red rocks
And from the top we'll see
The tall cliffs, the straight cliffs,
The fluted cliffs,
Where the eagles live.
We'll see the dark rocks,
The smooth rocks,
That hold the rain to give us
Water, when we eat our bread and meat,
When the sun is high.
Little spotted dog of mine,
Come and spend the day with me.
When the sun is going down
Behind the pointed hill,
We will follow home the flock.
They will lead the way
To the hogans where the fires burn
And the square cornbread is in the ashes,
Waiting our return.

Little Puppy
from the Navajo Indian
transcribed by Hilda Faunce Wetherill

6

Work dogs and
show dogs

Smudgie

by Oren Lyons

She was a lot of dog. When I first saw her some
kids were teasing her, throwing stones at her.
She was tied up behind my friend's house on a
chain and she was barking.

I didn't know what kind of a dog she was, but
I knew she was a different type from the ones I
was used to. Most of our Indian dogs are sort
of mixed up, mongrels I guess. This dog was
different. She was black and white and big with
a bony tail like a whip, big ears and a square
face and big chest. She was a lot of dog, with
something special about her.

So I used to come by and take a look at her and
one day I happened to see the fellow who owned
her and I asked him about her, "Where did you
get that dog? Where did she come from?"

"Oh, friend of mine downtown asked me if I
wanted a dog and I said 'yeah.' He said he couldn't
do much with her. So, I took her but I can't do
anything with her either."

I said, "She probably needs some running. She probably needs to be let loose off the chain."

"Yeah," he said, "but I haven't got the time to take her out. You can have her if you want. You can keep her, if you can feed her, because I can't do anything with her. She's just been tied like that for the last few weeks and it's not doing her any good and it's not doing me any good."

Well, I didn't expect that; the idea of owning a special breed of dog was really something I hadn't expected and I was very excited about it. Immediately I said, "Well, let me go back there." And I went back in the yard to take a close look at her. She was lying down beside her little house. Her chain was loose and she was watching me. I could see her tail wag a little bit. I said to myself, "Well, what she really needs is to get out and run," so I unhooked her chain and brought her over to my house.

I used to hunt a lot and we used to live off my gun. And I was a very good hunter. Whatever I didn't sell, we'd eat. We fed up on rabbits, deer, and pheasant. I had six brothers and one sister, plus my mother, and that's a lot of mouths to feed. I was the oldest one and my dad was dead so that a lot of this stuff fell on me.

I was a very good shot. I had this single-shot twelve-gauge shotgun my father used to use. I don't know where he got it. It was true. It would shoot straight. And, like I said, I was a very good shot. I had to be. I couldn't afford missing, couldn't afford wasting a shot because bullets cost a lot and we never had much cash.

I went in the house, got my shotgun, and said, "Well, we'll go and see." I got a long piece of rope and I tied one end on to the chain and I tied the other end around my stomach and we went off into the fields.

And she did want to run. And she did run. And
we ran together. I went every place that I could
think of that might have a pheasant or some kind
of a bird, but I couldn't get any good shots because
every time a bird would fly up she'd jump at it
and spin me around so I'd miss my shot. Anyway,
she wasn't afraid of the gun noise. She wasn't
gun shy and she really liked chasing birds.

And so we did this every morning. I'd get up
very early, grab a quick bite and go outside. She'd
be waiting. I'd put the rope on and off we'd go.
I would walk her until dark. We were both tired
by then. We both would just barely get back. And
she began to get the idea of the gun, the hunting,
and myself, and put it all together in her head.

Well, there came a time when I said I couldn't
be walking around with this rope around me
forever and I was going to have to unchain her,

and let her loose, and let her run. Either she was
going to stay or she was going to go.

By this time, we were getting to be pretty
good friends. She wagged her tail and she knew
me. She had nice eyes—brown eyes—and she
watched me very closely and I could tell a lot by
her eyes, what she was thinking and what she
wanted. So I figured today was the day.

I went out behind the house with her, down
into the fields, down across the creek, up to the
woods to the top of the hill, and then out on the
high flats where I knew there were birds. Well,
we got up to the flats and I still had the rope tied
on her. We got to a certain place where the grass
was high, and there was sumac and sassafras
growing nearby. The tall grass was next to a
cornfield and there were always birds in there—
pheasants. I figured, I'll take her in that way. So

we stood there at the edge of this huge field, this big flat area, and I was looking at this piece of land that I wanted to cover for birds and I said, "Well, Smudgie, I think I'm gonna let you go."

I don't know how she got the name. I always wanted my dog to have a good name, a fine name like Bullet or Wolf or Lobo or something of that nature but for some reason or other I'd just begun to call her Smudgie. Sometimes I called her Smudgepot. I guess I gave her the name because she was black and white, I don't know. But it seemed to fit her all right. I said, "Come here, Smudgie," and I pulled her over to me and I untied the rope.

"Okay, girl, you can go now. There's the field, there are the birds. Go huntin', you're on your own. Go!"

She didn't move. She really didn't understand that she was loose and free. She kept feeling it a little bit more each minute. She walked around me, looking at me all the time. Then she took a few steps here and there and started to jump around. She was a young dog. She couldn't have been more than nine or ten months at this point. She was a puppy yet really, but big.

And then she began running, running in wider and wider circles, and I could see her jumping, jumping up above the high grass. I could see her bouncing around. And then she took off.

She took off and ran and ran and I said, "Uh oh, there she goes," and she ran right out of sight, right over the hills and the knolls and right out of sight she went, and I said, "Well, she's gone." After all this trouble she'd run away.

"Well, I'll go huntin' myself," I said. "I'll go over there myself." So I started across the fields, keeping an eye out. After about ten minutes I could see her coming back. She was jumping through the grass coming back looking for me. Sure enough, sure enough, she came back, came all the way back. She came running up to me with her tongue hanging out, panting hard and her sides heaving from the long run. She was wagging her tail and looking at me asking if she did right. I didn't say anything at first. Finally I said, "Well, Smudgepot, you decided to come back. Well, that's good. You gonna work? You gonna hunt? You all through runnin' around? Come on, girl, let's go."

I started across the field and she came right along with me, moving just ahead of me. "Gee," I thought, "that's great, that's great, she's not running ahead of me too much and not scarin' anything off." So I moved along with her.

Well, we came out into this cornfield where the corn had been cut and a lot of it was down. We walked between the rows and I wasn't thinking of birds right there because it was so open. Usually you had to get over into the high grass before you could chase up a bird, especially this time of day. It was somewhere around ten-thirty in the morning, eleven o'clock. The birds would be through feeding and were probably back into their heavy cover.

We were walking along and Smudgie was walking in front of me by about ten feet. And all of a sudden I saw her freeze and stop still. And I stopped too. I said, "Now what's the matter with her?" I was looking at her and she had one front foot planted and one front foot was up in the air. She had pulled it up right next to her chest and her head was down and her tail was out and she was shivering, she was shaking, and I said, "Now what in the heck is the matter with her? She must have stepped on something to put her foot up in the air like that."

So I went over to her slow because she was acting so peculiar. And as I moved in next to her I looked in front of her and about four or five feet from her nose was this bird: a pheasant. It was sitting under a couple of stalks of corn that were down, hiding. And it took me a few minutes or a few seconds to realize that that's what Smudgie was looking at. That's what her nose was pointing at—at this pheasant. She was pointing at this pheasant! And then it began to dawn on me that Smudgie was a Pointer. She must be one of those pedigreed hunting dogs. On the reservation we were not used to having these kinds of pedigreed dogs. I never thought I'd see one, much less own one, but here sure in heck something was going on, because I had never seen a dog act like this before in all my years as a hunter.

I was about fourteen years old then, or maybe fifteen, I don't remember now. But I was a pretty good hunter. I'd hunted all my life. And I always had a dog and they were always good dogs but they always chased the birds and I had to run with them in order to get my shot. I never saw anything like the way Smudgie was acting. It was amazing!

Well, we stood there for a while. I must have been at least two minutes watching her, trying to figure it all out. Seeing her do this gave me a great feeling. It was something I had never seen before and I was enjoying it. "Boy," I said, "this is really great. Just look at her!" She had that bird really pinned and it was sitting right there and not moving a muscle. And I said, "Well, we can't stay here forever."

So I took a step and the bird flushed. Took off and flew right straight in front of me. When the bird took off my gun was up and I was already sighting down the barrel and I saw the bird winging straight up and then swinging to the right. It was just cutting to the right and I let go. BAM!

It curled up in a ball of feathers and came right down. It was a good shot, a dead kill.

Smudgie had been watching everything without moving and when the bird came down she took off like a shot. I said, "Uh oh, get back here! Come back here! Get back here!" But she wouldn't listen to me. Like a shot she streaked right over to where the bird was and I thought now she's going to pick it up and run away with it and eat the son of a gun.

She picked the bird up, turned around and came trotting back to me, with the bird in her mouth. And I couldn't believe this. I just stood there with my mouth open watching her come back and she had this sort of silly dog grin. The corners of her mouth were up and her ears were down and she came over wagging her tail. She came right up to me with the bird and I reached down and I took the bird out of her mouth and I said, "Thanks, girl. Wow, wow, what kind of a dog are you? What kind of an animal are you? You point at the bird and then you go and you get it." I couldn't believe it. I said, "Now this is some kinda dog."

Still I wasn't sure she'd do it again so I said, "Come on, let's go, let's find another bird. Let's see what you do this time." So we went down to the end of the lot, down into the fields, down into the heavy grass, and I watched her close. We weren't even ten feet into the grass when she came up on another point. She did the very same thing she had before. She held one foot up in the air and pointed straight ahead. I said, "Now, I'll betcha there's a bird there."

I watched her in the point for a minute. Then I came in behind her and started talking to her. I said, "Steady girl, whoa," and I walked in next to her. I couldn't see any bird because the grass was too heavy. So I walked past her and sure enough up flushed a big cock rooster, and he was hollering and cackling when he took off. And he took a quick swing. He swung out toward the left back over the field. He was flying up trying to get up over some small trees. I let go. BAM! Down he came. And Smudgie took off. As soon as he came down she took off like a streak. Through the grass, right over the fence, beyond the trees. I could see all the bushes moving where he had fallen down.

Then I could see her coming back, bouncing through the tall grass. She had the bird in her mouth and I couldn't believe it, and I said, "This is somethin' else. This is unbelievable!" I just was dumbfounded and I laughed and I grabbed her ears and I looked at her and I said, "Hey, now, are we ever gonna hunt, are we ever gonna hunt, you an' I." And she bounced around and she never bothered the bird. I picked it up and hung it on my belt with the first one and that day I think we got something like six birds.

We were a tough combination. We used to go hunting all over those hills. It got to the point that we communicated from way across a field. She would be on the far side of a field and I could raise my hand up and I could point in a direction and she would go over there. I could call her back and I could move her about just with my hand signals. I trusted her and she trusted me and we hunted.

We hunted in all seasons. I don't know how many hours and how many days, months or years we hunted together, but they were good years.

About the author   Oren Lyons is a chief of the Turtle Clan of the Onondaga Nation, one of the six nations of the Iroquois Confederacy. His Indian name is *Jo-agquis-ho*, which means "bright sun rays making a path in the snow." In addition to writing and illustrating *Dog Story*, the book from which this story was taken, he has also illustrated *Jimmy Yellow Hawk* and *High Elk's Treasure*, both by the Sioux author, Virginia Driving Hawk Sneve.

This yellow Labrador is a very special kind of dog. It is a guide dog, trained to lead its blind mistress safely through crowded city streets.

The extra-special dog

If you love dogs, all dogs are special. But some dogs work at a job that makes them extra special. These dogs are more than companions or protectors. They are the eyes for someone who can't see. We call these dogs "guide dogs," or "seeing eye dogs."

The first kind of dog trained for this important work was the German Shepherd Dog. But today, many other breeds are also trained as guide dogs. You may see a Labrador Retriever, Doberman Pinscher, Golden Retriever, Boxer, Border Collie, or other breed of dog guiding a blind person.

There are several groups that train guide dogs. Some breed their own dogs, some accept dogs as gifts, some buy dogs, and some get dogs in all of these ways.

A guide dog must be smart, gentle, and easy to groom. As a rule, a smart dog learns quickly and is easy to train. A dog that is to live with a blind person must be gentle. And, because its master or mistress is blind, the dog must be easy to groom and care for.

How does a dog become a guide dog? Each of many different guide dog groups has slightly different training methods. Here's what happens at one school where purebred dogs are bred and trained for this work.

When a puppy is about seven weeks old, it is given a number of tests to see if it is likely to make a good guide dog. How does it react to a collar and leash? Does it tend to come when called? Is it startled if someone jumps in front of it? How does it react to walking on different kinds of surfaces, such as metal, gravel, or wire screening? Is it willing to try going up and down stairs? Does it show a desire to fetch things?

There are good reasons for these and other tests of this kind. If the puppy is willing to come when called, it is likely to respond willingly to actual training. If the puppy is not frightened by sudden movement or by walking on a strange surface, it is not likely to jump or run when it comes up against a strange situation on the street. And if the puppy wants to retrieve, it should not be too difficult to teach it to bring its owner anything that the owner has dropped.

If the puppy passes these tests, it's ready for the next step. At about twelve weeks of age, the pup goes to live with a carefully selected family. During the next nine months, the dog will learn what life is like outside the kennel. It will have a chance to get used to the many strange sights and sounds of the world.

When it is about four months old, the puppy

A Golden Retriever, being trained as a guide dog, is taught to stop at a curb.

A young German Shepherd Dog is taught to obey the command "fetch!"

During part of a guide dog's training, the trainers wear blindfolds. They depend upon the dogs to lead them around things that are in their way.

starts at obedience school. Now it will learn to respond to such commands as *come, forward, sit, stand, down,* and *stay.* It will also learn to heel on and off a leash, to stay in position during left and right turns, and to retrieve on command.

At about one year of age, the dog is returned to the kennel. There, a trainer begins the real task of training the dog for its life's work. This training takes from three to five months. After a review of all the basic commands, the dog is fitted with a harness that has a U-shaped handle. The dog will wear the harness for most of its life.

Holding the handle and leash, the trainer puts the dog through every kind of experience it will have with a sightless person.

The trainer takes the guide dog into all kinds

of crowded places—on the street, in stores, in restaurants, and public buildings. The dog and its trainer walk up and down stairs and go up and down in elevators. They go through regular doors and swinging doors. The dog is taught to stop at a curb, as a warning that the handler must step up or down. And the dog learns to be alert for things it can walk beneath, but the trainer can't.

The guide dog also learns to wait for traffic to stop before crossing a street. If the trainer commands the dog to do something that might be dangerous, such as crossing when a car is turning

This German Shepherd Dog is taking a final test with a blind person. The trainer is there to watch the dog work and to prevent accidents.

a corner, the guide dog is taught then and there to disobey. It learns to wait until it's safe. Then the dog moves forward, leading the trainer who is guided by the movement of the U-shaped handle. In the last days of training, the trainer is blindfolded. Then it's completely up to the guide dog to see that all goes safely.

Now the guide dog is ready to meet the blind person who will become its master or mistress. Both the dog and the blind person go through four weeks of training, under the watchful eye of the trainer. After the four weeks have been successfully spent getting the dog and the blind person used to each other, they go home and begin a new life together.

A guide dog works for an average of eight years. During this time, it must be healthy and alert. The dog's hearing must always be sharp. If a dog starts to lose its hearing, or anything else goes wrong, the dog is returned to the school. Then the blind person applies for a new dog and starts all over again.

What happens to the "old" dog? People at the school find it a good home, where it can spend the rest of its days taking life easy.

The next time you see a guide dog leading someone down the street, watch the way the dog works. You'll soon know that you are watching a dog that is extra special!

A German Shepherd guide dog leads his blind master down a flight of steps from an airplane. Thanks to their well-trained guide dogs, blind people can enjoy more normal, happy lives.

It's plain to see that this police officer and his German Shepherd patrol dog love and respect each other.

A patrol dog lives with its master's family. When not on duty, the dog is a family pet.

Crime fighters

It was early morning, and in the kitchen of a house in Chicago a family was having breakfast. The husband and wife talked as they sipped their cups of coffee. The children giggled as they discussed happenings at school.

Lying near the man's feet was a big, handsome German Shepherd Dog. The dog's intelligent eyes followed every movement at the table.

The man finished his coffee, pushed back his chair, and stood up. He slipped into a jacket, put on a cap, and kissed his wife and children. As he headed for the door, the dog rose to its feet and followed him. At the door, the man snapped on the dog's leash and they went out together.

They might have been any man and any dog going for an early morning walk. But not in this case. They were going to work, *together*. The man was a police officer, and the dog was a police dog.

In a short while, man and dog would be at work patrolling in a park, or at a beach, or at an elevated-train station. By being in these places, they might well prevent a crime.

Police forces in all parts of the world use trained dogs to help with police work. Police dogs can do many things that a police officer can't do. They can go into pitch-dark places and their keen noses will quickly lead them to where a criminal is hiding.

Dogs can run much faster than any man, so they can chase and catch a criminal who is running away. The dogs are trained to corner a suspect, or to grab an arm or leg and hold on, until an officer can make the arrest. Police dogs can track down criminals, search out hidden evidence, and find lost children or injured people. Some of the dogs are trained to sniff out drugs and explosives.

Of course, it takes a lot of training to turn a dog into a police dog. And not just any dog can be used for this work. Most police dogs are German Shepherds. These dogs are smart, strong, brave, and big enough to either gently help a small child or terrify a desperate criminal. But other breeds, including the Doberman Pinscher, Bloodhound, Boxer, Airedale Terrier, and Labrador Retriever are often used for police work.

A police dog's training usually begins when the dog is about a year old. The dog must pass tests to make sure that it is healthy, intelligent, and neither shy nor savage. Then the training starts.

The dog, and the police officer who will be his master, are trained together. The dog learns to obey only his master. The dog is taught to climb ladders, leap high walls, go through windows, crawl into tight places and not to fear fire. He is trained to catch criminals without hurting them, to search for things, and to call his master by barking when he finds what he is searching for.

When the training is over, the dog and his police officer master are partners. They have learned to love and trust each other. From then on, the dog lives at the officer's home and is one of the family. Each day, the officer and dog work together to protect people and prevent crime.

A detector dog, working at an airport, sniffs freight for hidden drugs or explosives. German Shepherds are one of several breeds trained for this special kind of work.

The police often use Bloodhounds to search for lost people.

On the track

This big, sad-looking dog with a wrinkled face is the detective of the dog world. It has the best sense of smell of any breed of dog.

With these clues, you probably know the dog is the Bloodhound. *Bloodhound* seems a strange name for such a gentle dog. There's nothing mean or bloodthirsty about this dog, so why do we call it a *bloodhound?*

Some people say that the name is short for "blooded hound." *Blooded* is a term used for animals, especially horses, that come from good stock. And the Bloodhound has been a purebred dog for about a thousand years.

Other people think that, long ago, the name may have referred to the owners, not to the dogs. At one time, only noble people—who thought their blood was better than the blood of common people—could own Bloodhounds. But one thing is certain. The name doesn't mean that these dogs like blood.

Some books and movies have given people the wrong idea about Bloodhounds. True, these dogs do have a fantastic sense of smell. And police do use these dogs to follow the trails of criminals. But Bloodhounds never search in howling packs as they sometimes do in movies.

Bloodhounds are almost always worked alone or, at most, in pairs. The Bloodhound doesn't yelp and howl when on the scent. It usually tracks quietly. And it will go on for as long as it can find the scent. In fact one dog followed a trail for 138 miles—and found the person! Another dog, one of the most famous of all Bloodhounds, was named Nick Carter, after a storybook detective. This dog successfully followed a trail that was four days old.

When a Bloodhound finds someone, it never attacks. It wags its tail! It's happy to find the person it was looking for. To the dog, there is no difference between a lost child and a criminal. The dog can tell the different scents of people, not the differences in people.

In the United States, the National Police Bloodhound Association has a regular training program. Each year, a few owners from all over the country are invited to bring their dogs. The dogs go through a three-day training session. These trained dogs are then available for any emergency. This may mean trailing an escaped criminal. But more often, the dogs are used to find people who are lost.

This shaggy Puli is rounding up sheep on a farm in Hungary.

Sheep dogs and cattle dogs

Many thousands of years ago, people began to breed and train dogs to help care for herds of sheep and cattle. And many kinds of dogs have had such jobs ever since.

For a long time, dogs that looked after flocks of sheep had to be both shepherds and warriors. They had to be big, fierce animals that could fight off wolves that might attack the sheep. But today, wolves are gone from most parts of the world. Sheep dogs are now bred for intelligence, speed, and the ability to work for long hours.

Sheep dogs are smart. To turn back a stray sheep, the dog chases after it, crouches before it, and glares at the sheep until it turns back to the flock. A good dog can even separate a particular sheep from the rest of the flock!

A sheep dog has to be able to work for hours, and is almost always on the move. When it takes a flock somewhere, the dog has to run back and forth around the sheep to keep them together and moving in the direction it wants them to go. This means that the dog will travel about five times the actual distance the flock is moved.

The dog most widely used for herding sheep today is the small, smart, tough Border Collie. But in Australia, where a lot of sheep are raised, the Australian Kelpie is also a favorite.

In the past, many kinds of dogs were bred for this work. Sometimes you can tell by the breed name which dogs were once sheep dogs and the country in which the breed was first developed. The German Shepherd Dog, the Old English Sheepdog, and the Belgian Sheepdog all once helped care for flocks of sheep. The Collie, bred in Scotland, and the Puli, Komondor, and Kuvasz, bred in Hungary, were sheep dogs, too.

Cattle dogs don't work quite the same way as sheep dogs. A cattle dog nips at the heels of cattle to make the animals do what is wanted. A cattle dog learns to spot which hind leg bears the animal's weight. The dog nips at that heel. The dog then has time to crouch down before the animal can shift its weight and kick.

Dogs bred to herd cattle include the Cardigan Welsh Corgi, the Pembroke Welsh Corgi, the Rottweiler, and the Australian Cattle Dog.

Using the backs of the sheep as a bridge, an Australian Kelpie crosses to the other side of the flock.

Acrobats and actors

As the band plays, a little brown pony begins to trot around the circus ring. Close beside the pony, running easily, is a German Shepherd Dog. Suddenly the trainer cracks his long whip. The next time round, the dog races up a small ramp and with a single bound lands on the pony's back! The ooh's and ah's of the crowd become a gasp as the dog slips! But the four-footed acrobat quickly balances himself and braces his feet. The crowd roars as the pony continues to circle the ring, with the dog perched proudly on its back.

There are performing dogs all over the world. You've probably seen dog acts in the circus, at a carnival, in the movies, or on television.

It takes a lot of training to turn a dog into an acrobat or an actor. And, as any dog trainer will tell you, it also takes a lot of love and patience. Acting in front of a camera is especially difficult. Because of the microphones the trainer can't give the dog voice commands. So the dog has to be trained to obey hand signals. And the trainer has to work behind the cameras, or off to the side, so as to stay out of the picture.

Many individual dogs have become movie and television stars. Perhaps the most famous one today is Lassie. Through the years there have been many Lassies. And, strange as it may seem, each Lassie has been a male.

The first Lassie was a Collie named Pal. One day, Pal's owner brought his dog to the training school run by Rudd Weatherwax, one of the best dog trainers in Hollywood. The owner wanted the trainer to break Pal of the habit of chasing motorcycles and barking all the time. Later, Pal's owner gave the dog to Mr. Weatherwax in payment for a bill. Rudd Weatherwax continued

Two circus clowns and their dogs get ready to perform. The large, shaggy-looking dog is really a Weimaraner dressed in a costume.

An acrobatic German Shepherd entertains boys and girls at the circus.

Benji is a small, shaggy mongrel who has appeared in movies and on television.

In the heart-warming movie Sounder, *the part of Sounder was played by a crossbred coonhound named Swampy.*

to train the dog. Pal became so good an actor, he won the part of Lassie in the movie *Lassie Come-Home.*

One of the first dogs to become a great movie star was a German Shepherd Dog by the name of Rin-Tin-Tin. Believe it or not, this dog was found in a German trench during World War I. Lieutenant Lee Duncan, the American soldier who found the puppy, named the dog after a little woolen doll that French girls gave to soldiers as good luck charms. He brought the dog home to America and trained it himself.

Rin-Tin-Tin made many movies. In fact, he became so popular, he helped make the German Shepherd Dog a favorite pet.

Another German Shepherd Dog starred as an

Army attack dog named Joe in the television series, "Run, Joe, Run." This dog, whose name is really Heinrich of Midvale, was named the German Shepherd Dog of the Year in 1975.

A small, shaggy mongrel named Benji has also won fame as an actor. This dog played in the television series, "Petticoat Junction." He also had a leading role in a movie with the same name as his—*Benji.*

A crossbred coonhound named Swampy is another movie dog. You may have seen him in the movie *Sounder.* In the movie, the dog Sounder shares the joys and sorrows of a black sharecropper's family.

Wherever they appear, performing dogs are always entertainment favorites.

187

Choosing champion dogs

A neighborhood dog show can be a lot of fun. Boys and girls spend hours grooming their pets and having them practice tricks. There may be prizes for the smartest dog, the biggest dog, the littlest dog, and so on. It's all in fun, and it makes no difference if the dogs are purebreds or pooches.

But a real dog show, the kind given by dog clubs, is a serious affair. The dogs in these shows must be purebreds. And the judges are people who really know about dogs.

In the United States, most dog shows are run under the rules of the American Kennel Club (AKC). There are two kinds of shows. One is the specialty show, which is limited to dogs of one breed or group of breeds. The other is called an all-breed show, in which any recognized breed of dog can be entered. You may also hear the term "bench show." At a bench show, the dogs must be present for the entire show. When not being judged, the dogs are kept in stalls on benches. This gives people a chance to see the dogs.

A dog show, or conformation show as it is usually called, is really a sort of beauty contest. The dogs are judged on how well they conform, or match up, to the different standards set for each breed. The judges rate each dog on such points as color, condition of coat, teeth, shape and size of body, right down to the way the dog carries its tail and how well it stands, walks, and trots.

The dogs are judged in steps. At the first step, there are five classes for the males (called dogs) and five classes for the females (called bitches) of each breed. The winner of each class gets a blue ribbon and goes on to the next step.

At the second step, the best of the five males is named "Winners Dog" and the best of the five females is named "Winners Bitch." These two get points toward their championships. It takes fifteen points, including two major shows under two different judges, to become a "Champion."

At the third step, the Winners Dog and Winners Bitch compete against each other and against any champions of that breed entered in the show. The winner of this judging is named "Best of Breed."

At a neighborhood dog show, every kind of dog—pooch or purebred—has a chance to win a prize for something.

The judging area at a major dog show is busier than a three-ring circus.

At a show for purebred dogs, two girls keep their Old English Sheepdog company as they wait for the judging.

Now the breeds in each of the six AKC groups
—Sporting Dogs, Hounds, Working Dogs, Terriers,
Toys, and Nonsporting Dogs—are judged. One
dog is picked as the best in each group. These six
dogs are then judged and the winner of this final
step is the dog that is "Best in Show."

The most important dog show in the United
States is the Westminster Kennel Club Show,
held once a year in New York City. In England,
the most important dog show is Cruft's, held
yearly in London.

Dog shows are more than just beauty contests.
Dog shows help people to improve the quality of
each breed. Many winners and champions are
picked for mating because there is a good chance
their offspring will be fine puppies. And, of course,
dog shows help to interest people in the different
breeds of dogs.

If you're ever lucky enough to own a puppy
whose mother or father was a champion, you can
be sure you have a fine dog. Perhaps your dog
will become a champion, too, and earn the right
to the title "Ch." before its name.

These anxious handlers are making last-minute checks as they get their Old English Sheepdogs ready for judging.

An Irish Setter soars gracefully over the broad jump at an obedience trial.

Degrees for dogs

It's exciting to watch a smart, well-behaved dog obey commands. That's what an obedience trial is all about. You can usually see obedience trials at dog shows.

In an obedience trial, dogs do a number of things to show how well-trained and obedient they are. Dogs that pass these trials are given degrees, or titles. If you'd like to enter your dog in an obedience trial, here's what your dog must be able to do.

The first title is Companion Dog (CD). There are six tests your dog has to pass to earn this title. Your dog must heel (follow at your left side) on and off a leash. It must stand quietly for examination and come when called. And it must first sit for one minute and then lie down for three minutes with you in sight.

Dogs that earn the title of Companion Dog may then try for Companion Dog Excellent (CDX). To win this title, your dog must pass other tests.

Your dog must come when called. But while it is coming, it must drop (lie down) instantly on your command. Your dog has to make an ordinary retrieve and a retrieve that includes jumping over a high fence. Your dog also has to jump over a long, low broad jump. And, finally, your dog must sit for three minutes and then lie down for five minutes while you go out of sight.

An obedient dog is a better companion and pet than a dog that does as it pleases. At the very least, your dog should come at once when you call, it should heel at your left side, and it should sit or lie down quietly when you want it to. Dogs are easily taught to do these things. But they must be *taught*.

Many dog clubs hold obedience training classes for dogs. All kinds of dogs, both purebreds and crossbreds, are welcome. Usually, the dogs learn one "lesson" a week, and go to school for ten or twelve weeks. If you want to have a well-trained dog, one that will obey you instantly, obedience classes can be a big help.

Field trials

At a dog show, purebred dogs of all kinds are judged on their looks. At an obedience trial, purebred dogs of all kinds are judged on how well they obey commands. But a field trial is for purebred hunting dogs only. Hunting dogs are judged on how well they work. There are different kinds of trials for each of the different breeds.

Beagles, Basset Hounds, and Dachshunds usually compete in pairs. Their job is to find and trail rabbits.

Pointers and setters hunt for hidden birds. These dogs work in pairs, moving well ahead of the hunters. They are judged on their air of eagerness, on the way they "point" when they find a bird, and their steadiness while the hunter is shooting.

When one dog finds a bird and points, the other dog must not interfere. It must come to a stop and remain motionless behind the first dog. This is called "honoring the point."

Spaniels have to find and flush birds. And the moment the bird flies up, the dog must drop to the ground while the hunter shoots. The dog watches alertly to see where the bird falls. Upon command, the dog then retrieves the bird.

Retrievers are tested on land and in the water. In a water trial, the dogs may have to make three retrieves in a single test. Live ducks are often used. The ducks are tied so they can't fly.

As the dog watches, three shots are fired into the air and three ducks are tossed into the water. On command, the retriever must leap into the water, swim to one of the ducks, and bring it back unharmed. The dog must then go back into the water instantly and, one at a time, retrieve the other two ducks.

At a field trial for bird dogs, the dogs are judged by their ability to find birds. This Irish Setter has just picked up the scent of a game bird.

At a field trial for retrievers, the dogs are judged by the way they find and retrieve birds. This Golden Retriever, soaking wet from its swim, proudly returns with a duck.

Another, harder test, is called a blind retrieve. In this test, a dead duck is hidden, perhaps on an island in a lake. The dog has not seen the bird fall and has no idea where it is. The dog's master simply points toward the island and commands, "Fetch!" The dog must follow signals until it is close enough to the bird to smell it. Once the bird is found, the dog must make a speedy retrieve.

A dog that does well in field trials can win the title of Field Champion.

Special events

When heavy snows begin to fall, it's time for the thrilling winter sport of sled-dog racing. Each year, from Alaska to New Hampshire, across the upper Midwest, and in Canada, there are some four hundred exciting sled-dog races.

There may be as many as two thousand dogs, mostly Siberian Huskies, Alaskan Malamutes, and Samoyeds, entered in one of these events. In most races there are five to nine dogs on a team. But in some races, the teams may have as many as fifteen dogs. The dogs are hitched in pairs, usually with a single lead dog at the head of the team. The lead dog is all-important, because the driver has no reins. He must control his team by shouted commands.

A sled-dog race is a speed contest. The teams go off one at a time, racing against the clock. The dogs have to pull a driver and sled over a trail that may be anywhere from ten to thirty miles (16 to 48 kilometers) long. A good team will average between twelve and twenty miles (19 to 32 kilometers) per hour.

At the shout of "Hike!" a team races off down the narrow trail. Soon, a red flag on the right warns of a right turn. The driver shouts "Gee!" and the team swings right. On they go, the dogs enjoying the race as much as the spectators. The driver spots a red flag on the left and a shout of "Haw!" turns the team to the left.

The finish line is just ahead. Now the driver snaps his short whip to get the dogs to go faster. He may snap the whip, but he is not allowed to whip the dogs. As the sled crosses the finish line,

Sled-dog racing is a popular winter sport in the northern United States and Canada.

a shout of "Whoa!" brings the team to a halt. The driver has done well, but just how well he won't know until the winning time is announced.

At least he has been lucky in one way. All of his dogs have finished in harness. Not one has pulled a muscle or come up lame. A driver must finish a race with all the dogs he starts with, even if it means carrying a dog on the sled.

Another special event for dog lovers is the sheep dog trial. At these trials, shepherds and their dogs show how well they work together. The dogs are all working sheep dogs—usually Border Collies. Some of these dogs would never win prizes for looks. But at a sheep dog trial, looks don't count. The dogs are judged only by how well they do their work. These dogs are trained to respond to voice commands, whistles, and hand signals.

At a sheep dog trial, the dog is sent out to gather a number of sheep that are some distance away. The dog must then drive all of the sheep through two or more gates, herd them into a small circle, and finally into a pen. At one point, the dog must also separate marked sheep from the rest of the flock. And all this must be done within a certain time limit.

Coursing, or sight hunting, has been a popular sport since ancient times. In a coursing event, two dogs at a time race after a hare or jack rabbit. Greyhounds, Salukis, Borzois, Afghans, and Whippets are the breeds most often used for coursing. At one time, coursing events were held in flat, open country. Now, many of these events are held inside fenced areas and the hares have a better chance to escape.

England's Waterloo Cup is the most important coursing event in the world. Another is the Irish Waterloo Cup. A famous Greyhound, Master

Three speedy Greyhounds streak toward the finish line at a dog-racing track.

McGrath, was a three-time winner of the Irish contest. This dog had a statue put up in his honor and his likeness stamped on the Irish sixpence.

Still another popular sport is dog racing. Dog races are held on an oval track about 550 yards (503 meters) long. There are usually eight dogs in a race. The dogs chase a mechanical rabbit that runs on an electric rail. Greyhounds compete in most dog races, but there are also races for Whippets. The Greyhounds can reach a speed of about forty miles (64 kilometers) per hour. The smaller Whippets are only a little slower.

When Noah, perceiving 'twas time to embark,
Persuaded the creatures to enter the Ark,
The dog, with a friendliness truly sublime,
Assisted in herding them. Two at a time
He drove in the elephants, zebras and gnus
Until they were packed like a boxful of screws,
The cat in the cupboard, the mouse on the shelf,
The bug in the crack; then he backed in himself.
But such was the lack of available space
He couldn't tuck all of him into the place;
So after the waters had flooded the plain
And down from the heavens fell blankets of rain
He stood with his muzzle thrust out through the door
The whole forty days of that terrible pour!
Because of which drenching, zoologists hold,
The nose of a healthy dog always is cold!

The Dog's Cold Nose
Arthur Guiterman

7

Dogs in myths and legends

The tinderbox

Adapted from the story
by Hans Christian Andersen

A young soldier came marching down the road,
left-right, left-right, as if he were on parade. A
knapsack was on his back and a sword hung at
his side. He had been in a war, and now he was
going home.

On the road he met an old witch. She was an
ugly creature, with a lower lip that hung down
over her chin. But she greeted him, cheerfully.

"Good evening, soldier. My, but you're a fine,
handsome lad! How would you like to have all
the money you want?"

"That would be wonderful, old witch!" he cried.

"Well, then," said she, "do you see that big tree
by the side of the road? It's hollow, and at the
top of the trunk is an opening you can climb into.
We'll tie a rope around your waist so I can pull
you back up when you're ready to come out."

"But what am I going to do inside the tree?"
asked the soldier.

The witch cackled with laughter. "Why, you're going to stuff your pockets with money, that's what you're going to do! You see, at the bottom of the tree you'll find a wide passage, lit by more than a hundred lamps. At the end of the passage you'll see three doors with keys in the locks. Open the first door and you'll find yourself in a room where there's a big chest on the floor. Now, there'll be a great dog with eyes as big as saucers sitting on the chest, but don't worry about him. You'll have my magic apron. Just spread it out on the floor. Then pick up the dog and set him down on the apron. He'll stay there while you open the chest. You will find that it is stuffed with copper coins.

"But if you like silver even better," the witch went on, "go to the next room. There you'll find another chest, guarded by a huge dog with eyes the size of millstones.[1] But don't worry about him. Just set him on my apron, as you did the other dog. Then you can take your time going through the chest. It's filled with silver coins.

"And if you don't care for silver, go on to the third room. The chest in that room is guarded by an even bigger dog with eyes as big around as the great Round Tower of Copenhagen! But just you spread out the apron, put the dog on it, and you can take what you want from the chest. And *that* chest is filled to the brim with gold!"

"It sounds easy enough," said the soldier. "But what do you get out of it, old witch? Whatever I bring out I'm to share with you, is that it?"

"Not at all," she replied. "The only thing I want is an old tinderbox[2] you'll find in one of the

---

[1] A millstone is a large stone wheel used for grinding corn or other grain.

[2] Before matches were invented, many people carried tinderboxes. A tinderbox contained flint and steel for making sparks, and a small amount of tinder, such as bits of cloth, that would catch fire easily.

rooms. My grandmother left it there by mistake once when she went into the tree."

"All right, then," said the soldier. "Tie the rope around my waist and in I'll go."

So the witch tied the rope around him and gave him her magic apron. The soldier scrambled up the tree and slipped into the opening in the trunk. He soon found himself in a wide passage lit by more than a hundred lamps, just as the witch had said.

He opened the first door. There sat the dog with eyes as large as saucers, staring at him as though it were amazed to see anyone.

"Good dog," said the soldier, and immediately spread the witch's apron on the floor. He picked up the dog and gently placed it on the apron. The

soldier then lifted the lid of the chest and began
to stuff copper coins into his pockets. Shutting
the lid, he lifted the dog and put it back on the
chest. Then he went on to the second room.

There sat an even bigger dog with eyes the
size of millstones.

"You had better not stare at me so hard, dog.
It will make your eyes weak," said the soldier,
cheerfully. He then spread out the apron and
placed the dog on it. When the soldier opened the
lid of this chest and saw all the dazzling silver
coins, he quickly emptied his pockets of copper
coins. Soon he had filled all of his pockets and his
knapsack with silver.

Next, he went to the third room. He stopped
short, just inside the door. The dog with eyes as
big around as the Round Tower was a rather
frightening sight. The dog was extremely large,
and its enormous eyes rolled around and around,
like wheels.

"Good evening," said the soldier, and bowed
respectfully, for he had never seen nor heard of
such a fantastic creature. But being a brave man,

he put the witch's apron on the floor and picked up the dog. After putting the dog on the apron, he opened the chest.

Oh! The gleaming gold winked and sparkled at him! There was enough gold in that chest to buy the whole city of Copenhagen, as well as all the cakes, candy, and toys in all the world. Quickly, the soldier emptied his knapsack and pockets of the silver coins and began to stuff gold coins into everything that would hold them—pockets, knapsack, boots, and even his hat. When he left the room, he could hardly walk he was carrying so much gold!

"Hello, old witch," he called up through the hollow tree. "You can pull me up, now."

"Have you got the tinderbox?" she called back.

"Bless my soul, I forgot all about that," the soldier admitted, and went back to get it. Then the witch began to pull him up.

But when he was halfway out of the hole at the top of the tree she stopped pulling. The soldier found himself stuck. "Help me out," he said.

"Give me the tinderbox," she demanded.

"I will as soon as I get out," he said, struggling to free himself. "What do you want with the rusty old thing, anyway?"

"That's none of your business," she snapped. "You have your money. Now, you give me the tinderbox or you can stay stuck in that tree till you rot!"

"Oh, is that so?" he said, angrily. "Well, I'll get out by myself. And I'll just keep the tinderbox to teach you a lesson!"

With a great deal of effort, he managed to pull himself out of the hole. Then he climbed down and went on his way without so much as a backward glance at the witch, standing in the road screaming at him.

He went straight to the nearest town and walked into the first fine hotel he came to. There he asked for the very best rooms in the place and ordered the most expensive dinner. After all, he was now a rich man.

The next day, the soldier bought himself some fine new clothes. Then he decided to learn about the town he was now living in. Servants at the hotel told him about all the places of amusement and things to see in the city. And they told him of their king, whom they didn't much like, and about the princess, his daughter, who was one of the most beautiful princesses in the world.

"I'd like to see her!" exclaimed the soldier.

"Oh, no one can see her," all the servants told him. "The king keeps her locked up in a great copper tower, surrounded by walls and guards. You see, it has been foretold that she will marry a common soldier who will then take the king's place—and the king doesn't want that!"

"That can't be very much fun for her," said the soldier, thoughtfully. "Poor girl. I'd surely like to see her."

Now he began to live the sort of happy life he had always dreamed about. He went to the theater, ate in the finest restaurants, and slept as late as he liked. He gave a great deal of money to poor people, because he knew very well how miserable it was to have no money.

But, as he was spending a great deal of money without making any more to take its place, he soon began to run short. At last, he had only a few coins left. He had to move from his beautiful rooms in the hotel to a tiny, shabby room in the attic of a dingy old house.

He could not even afford to buy a candle for himself. But one evening, when he was wishing for light, he remembered the tinderbox. He could

make a little fire with that. He opened the box and began to strike the piece of flint against the steel. But no sooner did he strike a shower of sparks than the door burst open. And there stood the dog with eyes as big as saucers! It was the same dog he had seen in the first room beneath the tree. "What is your command, master?" the dog asked.

"Well, this is really something!" exclaimed the soldier in amazement. "Do you mean to say this tinderbox will give me anything I want? Bring me some money, then!"

At once, the dog vanished. An instant later he was back, with a large bag full of copper coins in his mouth. The soldier soon realized just how the tinderbox worked. If he struck the flint and steel together only once, the dog with eyes as big as saucers would appear. If he struck twice, the dog with eyes the size of millstones would come. And if three times, the giant dog with eyes the size of the Round Tower would be his visitor. Now the soldier knew he could have all the copper, silver, or gold coins he needed.

So the soldier moved back into his fine rooms at the hotel, bought new clothes, and began to live as he had before.

But one evening he began to think once again about the princess. Was she really and truly the most beautiful princess in the world? And he felt sorry to think of her locked up in the great copper tower, no better off than a prisoner in a jail. He did so wish he could see her.

Then, suddenly, he thought of the magic of the tinderbox. The great dogs would obey his every command. He struck the flint and steel together. When the dog with eyes like saucers appeared, the soldier said, "I know it's very late, but I want to see the princess—just for a minute."

Before he could even blink, the dog vanished and reappeared. Seated on his back, still sound asleep, was the princess. She was, indeed, very beautiful—not only the most beautiful princess in all the world, thought the soldier, but surely, the most beautiful *girl* in the whole world! He knelt down and very softly kissed her hand. Then, the dog whisked her away.

The next morning, it happened that the king and queen went to visit the princess in the great copper tower and she told them of a strange dream she had had. She dreamed that she had ridden on the back of a big dog with eyes the size of saucers, and that a handsome young soldier had kissed her hand.

"That's not a very proper dream at all!" the queen exclaimed. As a matter of fact, the queen wasn't so sure it *was* a dream so, just to be on the safe side, she had one of the ladies of her court stay by the princess's bed that night, to see if anything happened.

The soldier had been thinking about the lovely princess all day. When night came at last, he commanded the dog to bring her to him again. The dog did, but the lady of the court who was watching the princess ran after him as he dashed through the streets with the princess on his back. The lady saw the dog carry the princess into a large house. Taking a piece of chalk from a pocket of her dress, she made a large white cross on the door. Then she hurried back to tell the king and queen what had happened.

The soldier kept the princess with him for only a minute. Then the dog carried her back to the great copper tower. But the dog noticed the white cross on the door. At once, he took a piece of white chalk and made a large cross on the door of every house in the town.

Early in the morning, the king, the queen, and a number of soldiers of the king's guard came to find the house where the princess had been.

"Here it is," exclaimed the king when he came to a door with a cross chalked on it.

"My dear, where are your eyes? This is the house," cried the queen, pointing to another door with a cross on it.

Then they saw that there were crosses on all the houses. They had to give up the search.

But the queen was a clever person. She was good for a lot more than just sitting on a throne and looking grand. She cut a piece of silk into strips, and sewed the strips together to make a little bag. She filled this bag with the very finest white flour she could find. After tying the bag to the princess's waist, she made a little hole in the bottom of the bag. Now, when the princess moved from her bed, the flour would fall out of the bag, a little at a time, and leave a trail.

By now the soldier was deeply in love with the princess. He wished desperately that he could marry her and take her out of her prison in the copper tower forever. That night the dog came again, to bring the princess to the soldier for just a moment. As the dog ran through the streets, he did not notice the flour silently streaming out of the bag and leaving a long trail of white.

The next morning, the king's soldiers followed the trail of flour up to the soldier's rooms. They seized the soldier and threw him into prison!

Oh, how dark and disheartening it was. And the jailer kept coming to remind the soldier that he was going to be hanged the next day!

When morning came, the soldier looked out through the narrow window of his cell. Dozens of people were hurrying past. They were all going to the place where the soldier was to be hanged.

As the soldier watched, a little boy in a leather apron came running past. He was a shoemaker's helper. Just as he came to the soldier's window, the boy's shoe came off and he stopped to put it on again.

"Hey, lad," cried the soldier. "There's no need to hurry. There'll be no hanging until *I* get there. But if you'll do me a favor I'll pay you well! Just run to my rooms and bring back a tinderbox that you'll find there."

The young boy was glad to make a bit of extra money, so he rushed off to the soldier's rooms. He was soon back with the tinderbox.

The hanging was to take place just outside the town. Almost everyone was there. A pair of beautiful thrones had been put up for the king and queen to sit on while they watched the poor soldier die.

The hangman was putting the rope around the soldier's neck when the soldier called out, "Your Majesties! Won't you give a dying man one last request? Just let me smoke a pipe of tobacco before I die. It will be the last pleasure I have in this world!"

The king could not refuse what he thought was a harmless request, so he nodded. The soldier took out his tinderbox, struck the flint and steel together once, twice, three times—and there were the three magical dogs, with eyes the size of saucers, millstones, and the Round Tower.

"Help me!" cried the soldier. "Don't let me be hanged!"

At once the dogs began to growl terribly. The dogs looked so fierce that all the king's soldiers threw down their weapons and ran away. The king and queen drew back in fear. For the first time in their wicked lives they were at someone else's mercy!

Now the people really did not like the king and queen. And many of them did not want to see the young soldier hanged. So they began to shout, "Good soldier, *you* shall be our king! And the princess in the copper tower shall be our queen!"

Then they took the soldier over to the royal carriage. As they drove to the palace, the three magical dogs bounded along beside the horses. The princess was quickly released from the great copper tower. She was delighted to become the queen, because she was tired of being a prisoner. She felt she could do things to help the town and its people if she were their ruler. She was happy to marry the soldier, too, because she had fallen in love with him in her dreams, and knew that he loved her.

So they were married. The wedding banquet lasted for eight days. The three magical dogs sat at the table with the soldier and the princess. And they watched everything with their great eyes—eyes as big as saucers, millstones, and the Round Tower.

About the author   Hans Christian Andersen died a little more than a hundred years ago. But he is still Denmark's most famous author, and his fairy tales are loved by children everywhere. "The Tinderbox" was one of his first stories. If you liked it, you may want to find a volume of his collected stories. And, if you haven't read "The Emperor's New Clothes," or "The Ugly Duckling," these two stories are in *Stories and Fables,* Volume 2 of *Childcraft.*

The gathering at Googoorewon

The Aborigines of Australia tell this tale of how dogs came to be. All this happened long, long ago, in the Dreamtime.

Baiame, the Great Spirit, decided to hold a meeting of all the people. So he commanded the tribes to gather in Googoorewon, the place of trees.

Soon the scattered tribes began to arrive. The Baiamul, or Black Swans, arrived shortly before the Du-mer, or Brown Pigeons. Then came the Wahn, or Crows; the Madhi, or Dogs; and many other tribes.

There was great rejoicing as old friends met. Gifts were exchanged. Fires were lighted. The tribes sang and danced. The excitement grew. Why had the Great Spirit called them together? Nobody knew.

At last, Baiame explained. "I have called you together to teach you how to prepare the young men for manhood," he said. "First you must clear a large space for the ceremony."

All but the Madhi, or Dogs, obeyed. The Madhi just stood around watching. At first, no one said anything. Everyone knew the Madhi were lazy. As time passed, the Madhi began to howl with laughter. Still no one paid them much attention.

Everyone knew the Madhi were empty-headed. But when the Madhi began to bark criticisms at the workers, the old medicine men warned them to stop. Instead, the Madhi became louder and sillier. As their bad manners grew worse, Baiame knew that he must punish them.

"You Madhi have not behaved like men," the Great Spirit said. "So, from now on, you will no longer be men. You can sit around and bark and howl all you want!"

One by one, the Madhi dropped to the ground on all fours. Their arms became legs. Their hands and feet became paws. They grew tails. Hair covered their bodies. When they tried to speak, they could only bark and growl, snap and snarl, whimper and whine. These strange new sounds frightened the Madhi. With their tails between their legs, they disappeared into the bush. The Madhi had become the first dogs.

The hound of Hades

Hercules was the greatest of all the many heroes
in Greek mythology. He is most famous for the
Twelve Labors, or difficult tasks, he performed
for his cousin, the king.

As his First Labor, Hercules killed a fierce lion.
He then wore the lion's skin as armor. During
the next ten years, Hercules performed ten even
more difficult tasks. Finally, for his last Labor—
the most difficult and dangerous of all—the king
told Hercules to bring him Cerberus, the fierce,
three-headed dog that guarded the gates of
Hades, the Kingdom of the Dead.

Cerberus was no ordinary watchdog. His job
was to keep people *in*, not out. So, when Hercules
reached the Kingdom of the Dead, Cerberus did
not even stir as Hercules entered the gates.

Hercules went directly to the god of the dead,
who was called Hades.

"What do you want?" asked Hades.

"I want to take Cerberus to show him to my
king," Hercules explained.

"He is yours," replied Hades. "But *only* if you
can take him with your bare hands."

Hercules returned to the gates. But as he
approached Cerberus, even the mighty Hercules
hesitated. Never had he seen such a monstrous
beast. The huge dog had three great heads and a
tail like that of a dragon. And around each throat
was a ring of hissing snakes.

As Hercules drew nearer, Cerberus leaped for his
throat. Hercules caught the dog in midair. He
circled his powerful arms around the dog's body
and squeezed hard. The snapping jaws reached
out to tear him apart, but Hercules was protected
by the magical lion skin he wore. Then, with a
mighty thrust, Hercules raised the choking beast

high overhead. And in this way he carried the terrible Cerberus out of the Kingdom of the Dead, all the way to the king's palace.

When he stood before the king, Hercules cried out, "I have completed the Twelfth Labor!" As he said this, he dropped Cerberus to the ground.

Instantly, the dog rushed at the king, who leaped to safety. "Enough!" the king shouted. "I have seen enough! Take that monster back where it belongs!"

Hercules obeyed at once. He had completed the Twelve Labors in twelve years. And from that time on, Cerberus has remained where he belongs—guarding the gates of Hades.

Shiro and the golden coins

Long ago, in Japan, there lived an old man and an old woman who had a dog named Shiro. They all lived together in a small house. Behind the house was a garden with a beautiful pine tree.

The old couple were poor, but their wants were few. All they asked was enough money to buy rice for themselves and Shiro. But each year their savings grew smaller. They began to worry. Soon they would have no money for rice. What would become of them and Shiro?

One morning, the old man and the old woman were working in the garden. Shiro followed them around, sniffing here and there. Then, suddenly, Shiro began barking and digging.

"Hush your barking," the old woman said. "Our neighbor will complain!"

But Shiro kept barking and digging until the old man went to see what the dog was after. The old man poked his digging stick into the soft earth and felt it strike something. In a very short time, he had uncovered a small box. When the old couple opened it, they saw to their amazement that it was full of golden coins. Here was enough money to buy rice for the rest of the year!

Their neighbor soon learned of their good fortune and was very jealous. He wanted gold, too. So he dug wherever Shiro sniffed. But he never found a thing. Finally, in a rage, he killed the dog and buried him under the pine tree in the old couple's garden.

The old couple cried when they discovered that Shiro was dead, but there was nothing they could do. Then, one night the ghost of Shiro appeared to them.

"You loved me and cared for me. Now I will take care of you," said Shiro's ghost. "Cut down the pine tree. Then mix some wood chips from the tree into a pot of rice." So saying, the ghost vanished.

The next day the old man chopped down the pine tree. The old woman made a pot of rice. Then they stirred wood chips from the tree into the rice.

"Look," cried the old woman, her eyes filled with wonder. "Each grain of rice is turning into a golden coin. We will have enough money for the rest of our lives."

The old couple smiled sadly as they thought of Shiro. Even in death, their faithful old dog had not forgotten them.

Why dogs and cats are not friends

by Frances Carpenter

Once upon a time, so the old stories say, dogs and cats lived at peace with one another. They were good friends. They hunted together across the fields. They ate together from the same dish in their master's house. They slept side by side, by the stove in his kitchen.

Even today, that is how it is with some dogs and cats. But everyone knows most strange dogs and strange cats do not like each other. Everyone knows what people mean when they talk about the "dog-and-cat" life of quarrelsome families.

I am not the only one who would like to know why two such splendid animals as dogs and cats cannot be friends. In all times and in all lands, people have tried to find out the reason. Now, in Latvia, they say it happened like this:

When the world was just made, Adam, the first man, had a dog and a cat. Adam had not yet had time to think up special names for his animals, so he called them just "Dog" and just "Cat." No doubt it was God who had told him what they were.

At first Dog and Cat were happy together. They were the best of friends. Where Dog went, Cat went. When Dog ate, Cat ate. There was never a growl from the dog, never a snarl from the cat. Adam was greatly pleased with the dog and the cat which God had made for him. He never even had to scold them.

Soon there were other dogs and cats. In those times, as now, dogs liked to hunt. It was their nature to kill and eat the small creatures they found in the woods. All the dogs went out hunting together. One day they forgot the food they were meant to eat. They killed a fine sheep. It was one of Adam's fattest sheep. And Adam was angry.

"I shall complain to God, who put you dogs on this earth," Adam cried. And he made all the dogs go along with him to the place where God sat in judgment over the wrongs of the world.

"These dogs have killed a fine sheep," Adam said to God. "They killed one of my fattest sheep, and they ate it up. They should be punished." Oh, Adam was angry, just as farmers today are angry when dogs run after their sheep.

God was angry too. His face was as dark as the storm clouds He sometimes sends across the sky. And the dogs were afraid.

"We were hungry, O God," the dogs said. Their heads hung down. Their tails were tucked tight between their legs. And they were trying to give some excuse for this wicked thing they had done.

"Hunger comes to all living things," God said. "It is true one must eat when he is hungry. But I have put food for all here on the earth. The food meant for the dog is the meat of the creatures that are down on the ground." By those words God meant, of course, the small beasts, like rabbits and squirrels, that run low on the ground. But one of the clever dogs saw that "down on the ground" might be taken two ways.

"Will you write it on paper?" the dog said to Adam. "Will you please write that dogs may eat any animals that are down on the ground?"

Well, when he was home again, Adam wrote on a paper the words God had spoken, that "dogs may eat animals down on the ground."

"Adam's own Dog shall keep this paper safely for us," the other dogs said. "Yes, Dog shall keep our paper for us until it is needed."

So Dog took the paper. At first he never let it out of his sight. He slept with it under his nose. He laid it down beside his bowl when he ate. He even took the paper with him out hunting.

It sometimes was hard to know what to do with the paper when a rabbit ran past him. And one day, when Dog came in from the woods, the paper was wet with rain.

"You had best put your precious paper away some place where it will keep dry," his friend, Cat, said to him.

"Yes, I shall have to put our paper away," Dog agreed. "But where can I put it where it will be dry? Where can I put it where it will not be lost?"

"I know the very place," Cat said to Dog. "Up on top of the master's stove, far back in a dark corner. It is warm and dry up there. Your paper will be out of the way of the broom, too."

You see, in old houses in Latvia, the great stove was built of thick bricks. It had a broad, flat, smooth top. Adam, himself, often slept on top of the stove when the weather was cold. The top of the brick stove was Cat's favorite napping place. Cat could easily jump to its warm top from the stool that stood beside it.

"Good! Good! You are wise, Cat." The dog was delighted. "Put my precious paper up there, far back in the corner, well out of sight." Dog could not jump so high himself. He had to let the cat put the paper away for him.

After that, Dog was free to hunt far and wide. Each day he went forth with the other dogs. Most days they found plenty of rabbits and squirrels. But sometimes the rabbits did not come out of their holes. Sometimes the squirrels did not come down out of their trees.

On one such day, the dogs came upon Adam's horse, taking a nap under a tree. One of the dogs was more wicked than the others. At the sight of the horse, he cried, "Here is good meat for the hungry. With so many of us, we could easily kill that horse before he gets up on his feet."

"But Adam will be angry if we kill his horse. God will be angry, too. God said we should take only the creatures that are down on the ground." The other dogs were afraid.

"Is not this horse down on the ground?" the sly dog replied. "Did it not say in our paper that we might eat creatures 'down on the ground'?"

Now those dogs knew well it was not right to eat a fine horse. Perhaps they were more hungry than usual. Or perhaps they went ahead just for the pleasure of doing something they should not. However it was, they ate up Adam's horse.

Oh, now indeed, Adam was angry. He sent Dog out to bring all the other dogs before him.

"You shall be soundly beaten for this," Adam said to the dogs. "If God does not punish you, I

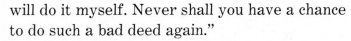

will do it myself. Never shall you have a chance to do such a bad deed again."

"But we have done no wrong," said the bold dog who had led the rest to kill the horse. "You yourself, Adam, wrote it on our paper. 'Dogs may eat animals down on the ground.' Your horse was such an animal. When we came upon him, he was truly down on the ground."

"God did not mean dogs to go around killing horses, any more than He meant they should kill sheep." Adam shook his head.

"Whatever He meant, that is what our paper says," the clever dog answered.

Adam scratched his head thoughtfully. He did not now remember just what the paper did say.

"Show me that paper," said Adam at last. "If the paper truly says that, I will not punish you."

"Dog, your own Dog, has the paper." All the dogs turned their eyes towards Adam's dog.

"I will go get the paper," Dog cried. And he hurried away to find his friend, Cat.

"Quick, Cat! Come quick! Climb up on the stove and get me our paper." Dog panted as he came galloping into the house.

Quickly Cat jumped up on top of the stove. With his paw, Cat reached far back into the dark corner where he had hidden the paper. But his paw found nothing at all that felt like the paper.

Cat pulled everything out where he could see it. But all he found was a soft paper nest, full of pink baby mice. Oh, it was a fine, soft nest for baby mice. For it was made of tiny, tiny—the very tiniest—bits of white paper. The mother mouse had nibbled them until one hardly could tell what the bits were. Alas, these bits of paper were all that was left of the precious writing Adam had given the dogs. Who could tell now what words there had been on that precious paper?

Cat timidly told Dog what the mice had done. Dog flew into a rage. He jumped toward the cat. And the cat ran fast as the wind, right out of Adam's house. Dog ran after the cat. And dogs have been chasing cats from that day to this.

Dog did not dare go back to the other dogs. He knew they would all jump upon him and tear him to pieces. No one ever saw Dog again. Ever since, all the other dogs have been looking for him.

Surely you have seen what happens whenever two strange dogs meet. They touch noses first. They sniff at each other. That is when the dogs are asking each other, "Are you Dog? Adam's Dog? Do you have our paper?"

Sometimes the strange dogs growl at each other. That is when they are saying, "No, indeed I am not Adam's Dog. Perhaps you are that dog yourself?" Then they call each other names. They may even fight.

Surely, too, you have seen a dog chase a cat up a tree. The dog barks and barks. He is scolding the cat for not having taken good care of the paper.

And when a cat snarls and spits at a dog, he surely is saying, "It was not my fault. It was the fault of the mice who chewed your paper to bits."

That is also the way Latvian grandmothers explain why both cats and dogs run after mice.

The dog and the fox

Diana, the beautiful Roman goddess of hunting,
had many dogs. Her biggest and strongest dog
was named Lelaps, which means "storm." And,
like the wind of a storm, Lelaps moved so fast
nothing could escape him.

Diana had a good friend, named Procris, who
was married to Cephalus, a hunter. Because she
wanted to help them, Diana gave them Lelaps.
She also gave Cephalus a magical spear that would
always hit the mark. With the aid of Lelaps and
the spear, Cephalus soon became a mighty hunter.

Now it happened that another goddess became angry with the people and sent a magical fox to pester them. Many hunters tried to catch this fox, but could not. The fox was so fast, no hound was able to follow it for long.

Finally, the hunters asked Cephalus for help. "Our hounds are not fast enough to catch this fox sent to pester us," the hunters said. "But Lelaps is as swift as the wind. He can catch the fox. And with your magical spear you can put an end to this fox once and for all."

As soon as Cephalus set Lelaps on the trail of the fox, the dog was off. Lelaps moved with such speed the hunters could not follow him. So they sat on a hillside to watch the chase.

The fox tried every trick. But no matter how fast the fox ran, or what tricks it used, Lelaps was always close behind. At last, the fox circled back near the hunters.

It was then that the gods decided to step into the affair. As Cephalus drew back his arm to hurl his spear—the spear that never missed its mark—both fox and dog were turned to stone. The gods had decided that neither dog nor fox should win.

The ribs of the dog

In northern Canada there is a tribe of Indians called the Dogrib. How did the Dogrib tribe get this unusual name?

There is a Dogrib legend that tells of a great quarrel among the people of long ago. After this quarrel, the people went their separate ways.

One Indian built a bark-covered tepee on the edge of a faraway lake. His only companion was his dog, who was expecting a litter. Before long, the puppies were born. They soon grew fat and playful, always eager to follow their master.

The Indian did not want the puppies to follow him into the forest, where they might get lost. So he made each of them a soft, strong collar and leash of buckskin. Whenever he went hunting, he tied the puppies to stakes inside the tepee.

One day as he was returning from the hunt, he heard strange sounds from the tepee. Instead of the barking of puppies, he heard the laughter and chatter of children! But when he entered the tepee he saw only the puppies, who fell over each other in their excitement to greet him.

The Indian was puzzled. Had he only imagined the laughter and voices of children? No, he was sure he had heard children. But where could they have gone?

The next morning, the Indian pretended to go fishing. But instead, he hid in the forest, close by. Soon, the barking of the puppies gave way to the laughter and chatter of children.

Carefully, so as not to make a sound, he crept up to the tepee and silently slipped inside. To his astonishment, he saw a group of happy children sitting in a circle about the fire. On the ground behind them lay the skins of the puppies. Before the spell could be broken, he grabbed the skins and threw them into the fire. And so the puppies who became children, remained children.

The children were the beginning of a new tribe. And from that day to this, these people have been known as the Dogrib Indians.

The faithful hound

Hundreds of years ago, in the country of Wales, there lived a young chieftain named Llewelyn.

Both great joy and great sorrow had come to Llewelyn. His pretty wife had given birth to a baby boy, but then she had died. For many long months, Llewelyn hardly left his stone house at the foot of Mount Snowdon. He spent most of his time just sitting and staring sadly into the fire.

In this time of sadness, his only companion was his dog Gelert. A strong, handsome hound, Gelert could run as fast as a flash of lightning. Llewelyn loved Gelert, and the huge dog adored his master. Gelert's greatest joy was to be at Llewelyn's side, both day and night.

The months passed, and time, at last, healed Llewelyn's great grief. There came a day when he looked out at the blue of the sky and the green of the forest and thought he would like to go hunting. In the past, hunting had been one of his great pleasures. And Gelert had always been with him. Oh, to know once more the joy of the chase, to see Gelert flying swift as the wind as they followed the deer! But this time, Gelert could not go.

"You must stay, Gelert" he told the dog. "You must keep watch over my son." Gelert whined, but thumped his tail on the floor to show that he understood. Llewelyn left the dog in the baby's room, stretched out beside the little bed in which the child lay sleeping.

Llewelyn spent most of the day hunting. But he had little luck. Most of all, he missed Gelert's company. Finally, he headed for home.

As he neared the house, Gelert came bounding out to greet him. But as the great hound leaped up with wildly wagging tail, Llewelyn saw with horror that the dog was red with blood! Blood dripped from his mouth and his coat was spotted with great red stains. What could have happened?

Fear clutching his heart, Llewelyn drew his sword and raced into the house. A trail of bloody paw prints led to the baby's room. As he entered the room, Llewelyn gave a gasp of dismay. The little bed was turned over on its side. A small blanket, now torn and smeared with blood, lay in a pile nearby. The floor and walls were spattered with blood. There was no sign of the baby.

With wild, horrified eyes, Llewelyn turned to look at the hound standing beside him. Gelert lifted his great bloody head and wagged his tail. Llewelyn knew what must have happened.

"Monster!" he roared. "You have killed my son!" Raising his sword, Llewelyn plunged it to the hilt into Gelert's body. With a shrill yelp of pain and surprise, the dog toppled onto his side. His pain-filled eyes stared up at his master. He seemed to be asking, "Why?" Then, death took him. His eyes grew dull and sightless, and his head sank to the floor.

As the enraged and grief-stricken Llewelyn stared down at the dog that had been his dearest friend and companion, he heard a small sound from somewhere in the room. It was the sort of sound a baby makes when it begins to wake up. And it seemed to come from beneath the torn and bloody blanket.

In an instant, Llewelyn snatched up the blanket. There, lying unharmed, was his baby son! And then he saw what he had not seen before. Behind the overturned bed lay the body of a huge wolf.

Now Llewelyn understood what had really happened. Somehow, the wolf had gotten into the house. And Gelert, brave Gelert, had fought it and killed it. The blood on Gelert, and on the floor, and on the blanket was the wolf's blood. Gelert had risked his life to save his master's baby—and Llewelyn had killed him.

Sobbing, the man picked up his son, turned, and knelt down beside the body of the faithful hound. The memory of Gelert's sad eyes staring at him in hurt bewilderment was like a knife in Llewelyn's heart. "Gelert," he wept, "you were the best of all dogs. How could I think you would betray your trust?"

Llewelyn buried the hound in a grassy spot near the house. Then he covered the grave with a high mound of stones, carefully piled together. Tears streaming from his eyes, he placed upon the stones the sword that had brought death to Gelert. And every evening at sunset, for the rest of his life, Llewelyn visited Gelert's grave. There he would stand, sadly honoring the memory of the brave dog that had saved his son's life—the faithful hound he had killed in a single moment of rash anger.

Perhaps one day you will visit the little Welsh village called Beddgelert—a name that means "Grave of Gelert." If so, you will see in a meadow a mound of piled-up rocks. People there say that this mound is the grave of Gelert, made long ago by the sorrowing Llewelyn.

I have no dog, but it must be
Somewhere there's one belongs to me—
A little chap with wagging tail,
And dark brown eyes that never quail,
But look you through, and through, and through,
With love unspeakable, but true.

Somewhere a little dog doth wait,
It may be by some garden gate,
With eyes alert and tail attent—
You know the kind of tail that's meant—
With stores of yelps of glad delight
To bid me welcome home at night.

Somewhere a little dog is seen,
His nose two shaggy paws between,
Flat on his stomach, one eye shut
Held fast in slumber, but
The other open, ready for
His master coming through the door.

My Dog
John Kendrick Bangs

8

You and your dog

Jack-in-the-Pulpit

by Lynn Hall

The sun had been up for only a short time, but already the grass was dried and the oppressive heat of an Iowa summer day was more reality than promise. In the backyard of the Methodist parsonage, the open cellar doors were stained sunrise pink.

I didn't notice the morning, though, as I came up into it from the dark cellar. My eyes, which usually had a nearsighted squint, were wide and unseeing with wonder. I was ten, but small for my age. My handed-down chenille bathrobe trailed in the grass. It flapped open at every step, exposing my horsehead-printed pajamas tucked into the tops of my cowboy boots.

As I crossed the backyard of the parsonage toward my own yard across the alley, my mind was still full of the miracle in the cellar. I barely noticed the Boston terrier from up the street, and he was one of my best friends.

Into the house I floated, heedlessly stiff-arming the screen door and letting it slam behind me. I was not a door slammer by nature. Mother glanced away from the tent-shaped toaster, opened her mouth to reprove me for the slam, then decided not to.

Deftly lowering the side walls of the toaster just before the bread began to burn, she asked, "Well, did they get born all right?"

"It was the most wonderful thing I ever saw in my whole life," I said in a high soft voice. "Thank you for letting me."

I sat down in front of the glass of orange juice, drained it, then went on in a voice more nearly normal.

"I didn't know they came out like that. Every time a puppy came out I cried, but it wasn't because I was sad or anything. Just because I was so excited. And Daisy didn't care a bit if I was there. She liked having me there. The puppies were in a kind of sack and Daisy took it off them so they could breathe and—"

"That's fine, honey, but I don't think we want to hear all those details at the breakfast table."

The minister's wife was a close family friend, and by prearrangement at my begging request, had called in the middle of the night to say that Daisy's pups were about to be born and if anyone wanted to watch he'd better come a-running. I had gone galloping across the dark backyards, had sat for three hours on an upturned coal bucket in the basement, had stroked the head of the homely little brindled dog between deliveries, had fought down my queasiness at the sight and smell of the birth, and had, for those few hours, held hands with God.

The rest of the family came in and knocked away the last of the holy mood—my father in his blue uniform that smelled of fuel oil; Jan, who was thirteen, beautiful, and omniscient; and Lois, who at five was already a more good-natured daughter than I could ever hope to be.

Jan asked, "Did you really get up in the middle of the night to see that dog have her puppies? You sure are crazy."

With this encouragement I repeated the account of the births, stopping just short of forbidden goriness.

Father said wearily, "Now I suppose she's got to have a puppy."

I glanced at Mother, my eyes wide with apprehension. I had been led to believe that the permission was secured. If Daddy said no now . . .

Mother said, "I told Lynn she could have one of these puppies IF she does all the work and the housebreaking and IF they aren't all spoken for. After all, Daisy's a sweet little dog, and short-haired, and I imagine at least some of the puppies will take after her."

My father sighed and acquiesced, but not without a final grumble. "You know what happens every time they bring a dog home. It wets all over the house, and just when they get attached to it, it gets run over or poisoned or something, and everybody bawls."

I got up and began easing toward the back door.

"No you don't." Mother cut me off. "The puppies will still be there this afternoon. You trot upstairs and take a nap."

That afternoon I resumed my seat on the coal bucket in the parsonage basement. The puppies were dry now, and nursing. With my parents' permission secured and this wealth of puppies from which to choose, I felt strung up with joy. I was studying the seven pups when the minister's wife came down the stairs from the house.

"Before you decide which one you want," she said, "I'd better tell you that all but two have been spoken for. The only ones left are that brindled one in the middle and the little black runt. You can't see him now. I guess he's on the bottom of the heap there somewhere."

With the field thus narrowed the choice was simple. I fished the tiny black puppy up from the bottom and held him reverently, close to my face. His mouse-sized claws swam against my hand, and the already-dried umbilical cord scratched my palm. I shivered and cupped my hands lovingly around him.

Laying the pup against my chest, I said, "I want this one. Did you pick out names for them yet?"

The minister's wife knelt beside the box. Daisy's tail struck the bedding. "Yes, we named them all after flowers. Because of Daisy. That one you've got is Bachelor Buttons. Let's see if I can remember the others—Marigold, Rosebud, Jack-in-the-Pulpit, Dandelion, what was that other one . . ."

But I heard nothing after Bachelor Buttons. Buttons. My dog. The others held no further interest. I stayed in the basement as long as I could, gave Buttons a long good-night cuddle, and went home reluctantly.

All through supper I talked about Buttons. No one listened, but I couldn't seem to stop. I was still on the subject when supper was over and I stood beside Jan, drying the dishes. Jan was preoccupied with things more important than newborn pups, but for once she was kind enough not to say "Shut up and wipe the dishes. You're getting on my nerves."

"I'm going to teach him opposite commands," I said, just as though someone were listening.

"You know, to lie down when you say 'Up' or to dance on his hind legs when you say 'Play dead.' It isn't any harder to train a dog to do opposite commands than—"

The phone rang. It was the minister's wife, talking to Mother. They were good friends and often called one another after supper, so I paid little attention until I heard "Yes, I'll tell her. No, I don't think so, just so she gets one of them. You'll be sure to save the other one for her, though? What? Jack-in-the-Pulpit? Well, that's appropriate." She laughed. "Listen, is our circle supposed to be in charge of the refreshments for Meyers' wedding, or . . ."

Bachelor Buttons was dead. I hardened my jaw and refused to cry in front of Jan. That's what I get for wanting the runt of the litter, I told myself bitterly. But there's still the other puppy. Ugly brindle color though, and an ugly name. Jack-in-the-pulpit . . . I dried a handful of silverware and dealt them into their partitioned drawer—knife, knife, fork, knife, spoon, spoon, fork. Jack-in-the-Pulpit.

The requisite six weeks could not have gone more slowly if they had been the last weeks of the school year. It was midsummer, and except for my regular chores of burning trash, cleaning my room, doing dishes, and mowing the lawn, my time was my own. Most of it was spent in the parsonage cellar.

The little brindle sausage was the first of the pups to show a slit of gleaming black eyeball. I knew it was because he was in a hurry to see me, and it was all the proof I needed that Jack was

the pick of the litter. By now the black puppy
was all but forgotten.

At last the six weeks were up and Jack and I
entered the nerve-strung weeks of housebreaking.
Because the cries of a lonesome puppy might
annoy the neighbors, I was instructed to keep the
pup indoors at night. I was more than willing
because I could hardly bear to be out of sight of
Jack, but the nights were nearly sleepless. Fear
kept me awake, fear of waking to find a puddle
or worse on the rug, fear of the ever-threatening
parental edict, "We just can't have this mess in
the house, Lynn. You'll have to get rid of him."

Four or five times a night I got up in haste,
pulled on my cowboy boots and bathrobe, and
snatched up Jack, who was bumbling and sniffing
around. Down the stairs we went on tiptoes, out
the side door and into the safety zone of the
grass. I sat on the concrete steps and watched
for action with eyes still reluctant to open and
focus. Then, back in bed with the puppy safely
drained, I was too roused by the night air to go
to sleep.

Sometimes my inner warning system failed to
wake me at the sound of Jack moving around,
and in my dream I'd hear an amplified torrent of
rushing water. I'd wake, heart hammering. The
light of the reading lamp would show the puddle
and Jack, head low, tail wagging tentatively
between his hocks.

Fortunately there was an upstairs bathroom
and my folks' bedroom was downstairs, so I was
able to mop things up undetected, unless the
accident happened on the rug. Then there was no
way to dry the spot, or to hide it, before morning.

Although I tried hard not to show it, the
post-accident tension I felt was impossible to
hide. Each morning I waited for Mother to go up

to my room, see the damp place on the rug, and say, "Well, this is it. We can't put up with this mess any longer, Lynn. He'll have to go."

But the words were never spoken. Gradually the accidents ceased to happen. By the time school started the danger was past.

Jack grew into a dog that could have been beautiful only to me. He was beagle-sized and beagle-shaped, but with no houndlike suppleness. He was rock-hard, with the musculature of a bull terrier. His toughness was belied, however, by the comic aspect of his ears. One stood upright, while the other drooped. When people laughed at him, I was torn between welcoming their laughter as a sign of affection toward my dog, and resenting it as ridicule.

In those days the small town where we lived had not yet been engulfed by the nearby city and transformed into a suburb. It was still surrounded by open fields and woods within easy reach of a girl on a bicycle, and a sturdy little brindled mutt.

The following summer Jack and I spent every

possible moment away by ourselves. For the first time I knew the heart-filling luxury of having a dependably loving companion. In Jack's company I was free to say foolish things, to act silly, to lie on the grass and roll down a long hill with my dog barking and nipping at my heels all the way down.

During cold weather we had to stay close to home, but fortunately the house was large enough to provide getting-away places where baby sisters couldn't follow. The best place was my room, because no one could come in without my permission, ever. There, with Jack curled against my legs, I could lie across the bed and lose myself for hours in my dog and horse books.

About the author   Before she started writing for children, Lynn Hall worked in a pet hospital and as a professional dog handler. You may want to read *Lynn Hall's Dog Stories*, from which this story was taken, or her other dog books, such as *Flash, Dog of Old Egypt, Kids and Dog Shows,* or *Stray.*

So you want a puppy

There's a lot more to getting a puppy than just saying you want one! And there are lots of ways to get one. Someone may give you a mixed breed. Perhaps you'll decide that you'd like to adopt a puppy at an animal shelter. Or, you may want to buy a purebred dog.

If you plan to buy a purebred dog, there are many things you will have to decide. What breed do you want? Do you want a dog with long hair or short hair? Do you want a male or a female? Do you want a big dog or a small dog?

Generally speaking, the Sporting Dogs, Hounds, and larger Working Dogs tend to be quieter than most of the Terriers and Toys. A dog with long hair will need more grooming than one with short hair. As a rule, females are less likely to roam than are males. Think about the dog's problems, too. Do you live in an apartment or in a house? Do you have a small yard or lots of land?

Shop around before you pick out a puppy. Find a good kennel that breeds the kind of dog you want. It's best to get a puppy that is between eight weeks and three months old.

Look the puppy over carefully. You want a pup that is healthy. Its eyes should be clear and bright. Its nose should be moist but not runny. How does the pup act? It should be friendly with you and its brothers and sisters. A very shy, unfriendly, or bad-tempered puppy is not likely to change its ways as it gets older.

Plan to take the puppy to a veterinarian right away for a complete checkup. So, find out what shots the puppy has had and what ones it needs. And, if you are buying a purebred dog, you'll want to find out about getting proper registration papers and a pedigree.

Like all puppies, these little Yorkshire Terriers are cute and lovable. Puppies are lots of fun, but they also mean a lot of work for someone.

Finally, unless you plan to breed or to show your dog, have it operated on so it can't have puppies. This should be done whether your dog is a male or a female. The operation won't hurt your dog or cause the dog to change in any way.

A puppy means a big change in your life. A puppy needs plenty of loving care. Puppies have "accidents." Are you ready to clean up after your puppy? All puppies love to chew on things. Will you watch the puppy and do your best to keep it out of trouble? You'll have a lot of work to do and you'll need lots of patience. But it's worth it—if you really want a puppy!

My puppy is born

Puppies don't grow like cabbages, all in a row. Puppies begin when a male and female dog are mated. The mother dog is called the dam. The father dog is called the sire. The puppies grow inside the dam. Each puppy gets food and oxygen through a tube that's attached to it and the dam. This tube is called an umbilical cord.

About two months after the dam and the sire are mated, the puppies are whelped, or born. The dam may have one puppy, a dozen puppies, or

A litter of healthy, hungry Chesapeake Bay Retriever pups, only four days old, take milk from their watchful mother.

*At four days of age, the pups spend all their time
sleeping and eating. They still cannot see or hear.*

even as many as twenty puppies. The newborn
puppies are called a litter.

Each puppy is born inside a see-through bag
called a sac. The dam tears open the sac, then
separates herself from the puppy by biting
through the umbilical cord. After this, she licks
the puppy until it starts to breathe and is clean
and dry.

The puppies snuggle against the warm body of
the dam and take milk from her. Their eyes are
closed and their ears are sealed. They won't be
able to see or hear anything until they're about
two weeks old.

Newborn puppies don't look much like the
dogs they will grow up to be. Dalmatian puppies,
for example, have no spots. These appear later.

When the puppies are about four to five weeks
old, it is time to start weaning them. Weaning

Now four weeks old, the puppies can see and hear all the
sights and sounds around them. And when let out to play, they
enjoy chasing after a ball on their fat, wobbly little legs.

At four weeks of age, the puppies are starting to take some solid food. But they will also nurse from their mother for about two more weeks.

simply means getting them used to food other than the dam's milk.

At first, the puppies are fed warm milk and baby cereal. When they are used to this, they are also given small bits of meat. During this time, the puppies continue to nurse from the dam.

By the time the puppies are about six weeks old, they will be completely weaned, or used to eating regular food. What's more, they will be wobbling about, sniffing at all the strange and wonderful smells around them.

During the next few months, the pups will grow quickly, becoming ever stronger and more active.

These two dogs look very different. The Basset Hound (above) has a long nose and big, floppy ears. The French Bulldog (right) has a short, pushed-in nose and big ears that stand straight up. But like all dogs, both have keen senses of smell and hearing.

From head to tail

When you want to find out about something, you take a close look. That's because you trust your eyes. But when a dog wants to find out about something, it takes a close smell. That's because a dog trusts its nose.

A dog's nose may be long and pointed, like that of a Poodle, or it may be pushed in, flat, and square, like that of a Bulldog. Most dogs' noses are black. But some are brown or pink. And some are spotted. But, whatever the color or shape of its nose, a dog's sense of smell is so keen it recognizes things by smell rather than by sight.

The tip of a dog's nose is usually cold and wet. The moisture comes from a gland inside the nose. The moisture helps the dog detect odors. A cold, moist nose is supposed to be a sign of a healthy dog, but a dog can have a warm, dry nose and still be perfectly healthy.

No two dogs have the same noseprints. A dog's noseprint identifies a dog the same way your fingerprints identify you.

A puppy is blind at birth. Its eyes open about the tenth day. But even when the puppy is fully grown, it will never see as well as you do.

Dogs see things first because of movement, second by brightness, and third by shape. And, for all practical purposes, dogs are color blind. And so, most dogs usually depend on their nose and ears more than their eyes.

Dogs' ears come in many shapes and sizes. Some dogs have ears that stand straight up. Some dogs have ears that hang down. And some dogs have ears that are partly folded over.

Next to its nose, a dog depends most on its ears. A dog can hear much better than you can. It can also hear very high-pitched sounds that you can't hear.

Some people use special whistles to call their dogs. You could blow with all your might on one of these whistles and not hear a sound. But a dog would hear it even at a great distance. But don't ever blow this kind of whistle when the dog is close to you. The high-pitched sound can be very painful to the dog.

A puppy is born without teeth, but soon gets thirty-two milk teeth. After about four or five months, the milk teeth begin to fall out as the permanent teeth grow in.

Grown dogs have forty-two teeth—ten more than you will have when you grow up. The front teeth, six in the upper jaw and six in the lower jaw, are the incisors. These are the biting teeth. The largest teeth are the four canine teeth, or fangs. These are used for holding and tearing. Other teeth, and strong jaw muscles, make it possible for a dog to crush bones.

*A Gordon Setter (above)
has a fairly long, slightly
wavy coat with feathering.
A smooth Fox Terrier (left)
has a short, flat coat that
hugs its body.*

If you watch a dog eat, you'll see that it gulps its food down instead of chewing it as you do. That's because a dog's teeth aren't made for chewing. The strong juices in a dog's stomach help to digest the big lumps of food.

Have you ever wondered why a dog always seems to have its tongue hanging out? It's a dog's way of cooling off. On a hot day, or after a good run, a dog needs extra air. So it sticks out its tongue and pants, or breathes heavily. This gives the dog the extra air it needs to cool off the inside of its body.

A dog's hairy covering is called a coat. This coat is like your clothes. Many dogs have two coats—an undercoat and an outercoat. The soft, dense undercoat keeps the dog warm during cold weather. In warm weather, the dog sheds, or loses, its undercoat. The outercoat protects the dog from rain and snow.

You can tell a lot about a dog's feelings just by watching its tail. When a dog is very pleased or excited, it will wag its tail madly. But when a dog is frightened or in pain, it tucks its tail between its legs.

A dog's tail is sometimes called a rudder. And dogs with long tails do use the tail as a rudder when swimming. Some breeds, though, have naturally short tails. And in other breeds, the tail is docked, or cut off short, when the puppies are about three days old.

Why is this done? Today, it's done to make the dog look more attractive. Long ago, however, it was done to avoid paying taxes. Dogs used to drive sheep and cattle to market—called drovers' dogs—were not taxed. Owners docked their dogs' tails to show the kind of work done by these dogs. That's how the Old English Sheepdog got its nickname "Bobtail."

The Parts of a Dog

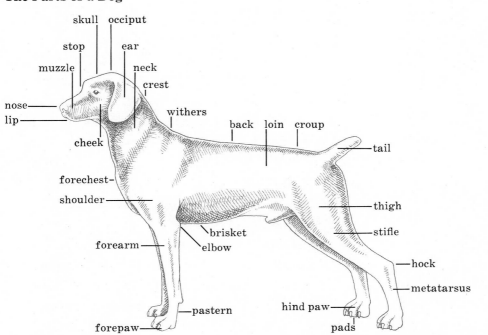

Feeding your dog and giving it fresh water are two jobs you should do yourself.

Feeding your dog

Your dog will need food and water every day of its life. A dog always needs water, so keep a bowl of fresh water out all the time. Food is a different story. Your dog will need different amounts and kinds at different ages.

Growing puppies need a high-quality diet and two to four meals a day. When you get your pup, ask about the kinds and amount of food it should have. And check with the veterinarian, your dog's own doctor, too.

When a dog is grown, one meal a day is quite enough. How much you feed your dog will depend on the size of the dog and the amount of exercise the dog gets. A good rule is to give the dog a little less food than it might like rather than too much. If your dog doesn't eat all its meal in a reasonable time, throw out what's left. And don't worry if your dog skips a meal once in a while. This is perfectly normal.

Never give your dog chicken bones, pork bones, or lamb bones. These bones splinter and the dog could get one caught in its throat. If you give the dog a bone, make it a big beef bone.

Make sure your dog's food and water dishes are kept clean. Germs are just as bad for dogs as they are for you.

A basket or a doghouse?

Will your dog live in your house, or outdoors in a house of its own?

If your dog is going to sleep in the house, fix a place away from drafts and radiators. A small dog does very nicely in a box or basket. A big dog can do very well with an old rug or blanket.

Dogs that are kept outside should have a safe, fenced-in area and a good doghouse. The floor of the doghouse should be off the ground to keep out the damp. The roof should be hinged to make the house easier to clean. A carpet or canvas flap over the opening will help keep out the wind and rain. For bedding, use cedar shavings, shredded newspapers, or old blankets.

Whether you keep your dog inside or outside be sure to keep the bedding fresh and clean.

A travel cage doubles as a bed for this bright-eyed Brussels Griffon.

Bathing and grooming

Lucky dog! It doesn't need a bath every day. In fact, too many baths can remove natural oils and make a dog's coat dry and harsh. So don't give your dog a bath unless he's really dirty or smelly.

Regular grooming is the best way to keep a dog clean and looking good. Dogs with short hair should be brushed. Dogs with long hair should be carefully combed and then brushed.

When you have to give your dog a bath, a laundry tub or bathtub is the best place to do it. To keep the dog from sliding about, put a bath mat or heavy towel in the tub. Stand the dog in the tub, plug its ears with cotton, and put a drop of mineral oil in each eye. This will protect the ears and eyes from soapy water.

Run in warm water up to about the middle of the dog's legs. Wet the dog and then work up a good lather with mild soap, a dog soap, or a dog shampoo. Work from the head toward the tail. When finished, be sure to rinse the dog well.

Wrap the dog in a big towel before he has a chance to shake himself. Rub the dog briskly until he is as dry as possible. Keep the dog out of drafts until he is completely dry. Then finish the job with a good combing and brushing.

To keep your dog looking its very best, you have to comb and brush its coat regularly. This is especially true of long-haired dogs such as this Afghan Hound.

Housebreaking your puppy

Housebreaking—teaching your new puppy not to go to the bathroom in the house—is the first step in training.

Until the pup is housebroken, keep him in one small part of the kitchen. Fix up a box for him and put down newspapers.

Take the pup for a walk the first thing in the morning and the last thing at night. Don't leave water out for him during the night. Take him out about an hour after each feeding. If possible, take him out if he even looks as if he has to go. And praise him when he does go outside!

When accidents happen—and they will—don't hit him. Just scold him with your voice. Say, "No! Bad dog!" If you can, take him out right away. And praise him whether he goes or not.

You may have to leave the pup alone for hours at a time. Or, if you live in an apartment house, you may not always be able to take him out as often as necessary. Either problem can be handled by paper-training him.

To do this, confine the pup to a corner of the kitchen and put down papers as before. After a few days, leave part of the floor bare. If the pup goes on the bare floor, scold him and put him on the papers. Praise him when he uses the papers. He'll soon learn to go on the papers if he can't get outside. In time, he'll be able to control himself between walks and you can take up the papers.

Housebreaking takes time and patience. Don't expect quick results. And don't give your pup the run of the house until he is housebroken. When you do allow him into other parts of the house, you'll have to teach him to leave things alone and to stay off the furniture. So keep a close eye on him during this training period.

Training your dog

A well-trained dog is a joy to see and a joy to own. When people watch your dog with wonder, you will feel a tremendous sense of pride.

Serious training should begin when your dog is about six months old. He'll be used to a collar and leash and will understand the meaning of "No!" And he'll be old enough to remember the things he is taught.

Before you begin the training, there are a few things you should know—and remember. When your dog doesn't do what you want, correct him instantly. Make sure he obeys *every* order you give. Correction may be a harsh "No!" or simply pushing him into the position you want.

Never strike your dog. And don't threaten him with your hand. He'll learn to see every upraised hand as a threat. And don't shout. He can hear. Praise your dog in a warm, friendly voice. Scold him in a harsh voice.

When you scold your dog is very important. Never scold him after you have called him to you or he has come to you himself. He'll think he's being scolded for coming, not for what he did before that. If he is some distance away when he does something wrong, just get him under control and start the lesson again.

A well-trained dog should know the six basic commands: heel; sit; stay; stand-stay; down; and come. The commands should be taught in that order. The dog must learn to obey instantly, after only one command.

Try to have two short training periods each day. Fifteen to thirty minutes is plenty of time. Any more and the dog may get restless. Find a quiet place, inside or outside, where the two of you can be alone. Keep the dog on the leash at all times so that he is under your control. Don't work him off the leash until he has mastered all six commands.

For training purposes, you'll want a chain or leather choke collar. This kind of collar tightens around the dog's throat when you give the leash a jerk or the dog tries to pull away. Never use constant pressure. A quick jerk and release will do the trick. Training is not a test of strength, it is a test of will.

When you start a lesson, say the dog's name first and then the command, as, "Rex, heel!" Use the dog's name to get his attention, so that he will be alert for the command.

Don't go to a new command until the dog has mastered the last one. If he has trouble, go back to the last command so that you can praise him. Always end a lesson with praise.

As training goes on, things will get easier. The dog will learn that a command means that he is to do something. He just has to learn what he is supposed to do. Training takes a lot of time and patience. But it is more than worth it. When your dog is trained, you will have a companion you can be proud of.

Heel: On this command, your dog should walk at your left side, about even with your left knee.

Snap on the leash. Take the free end in your right hand. With your left hand, hold the leash near the collar so that the dog has to walk close to you.

As you start forward, say, "Rex, heel!" On the word, "Heel!" give the leash a quick jerk. If the dog starts to move ahead or lag behind, give the leash a quick jerk and say "Heel!" When the dog is back in position, praise him. Never pull, or allow him to pull, on the leash. Just use a quick jerk and then release the pressure.

With practice, your dog will stay by your left knee as you walk, trot, make turns, and go in circles. In time, your dog will heel on or off the leash. When he has mastered the heel, go on to the sit.

Sit: The sit should be taught while your dog is heeling. He should learn to sit, without command, the moment you stop.

Walk with your dog at heel. Reach over with your right hand and grasp the leash just below your left hand. Take your left hand off the leash. Then stop and give the command, "Sit!" At the same time, pull up on the leash with your right hand and push down on the dog's hindquarters with your left hand.

Hold the dog in this position for a moment and praise him. Then give the command to heel and start walking. After a few steps, repeat the sit. As he begins to get the idea, you can stop giving him the command to sit. Finally, you can stop guiding him with your hand and the leash.

When he will sit, without command or help, the instant you stop walking, you can begin teaching him to sit on command from any position.

Stand the dog in front of you, close to your legs, and give the command to sit. As before, guide him with your left hand and the leash. When he has mastered the sit at heel or from any other position, you can introduce the command to stay.

Stay: The command to stay should be taught while your dog is sitting. In the stay, your dog must sit without moving until you give him another command.

Snap on the leash and command the dog to sit. Then, hold your hand up in front of his nose and in a firm voice say, "Stay!" Repeat the command. If necessary, use your hands to hold the dog in position.

The first few times, don't make the dog stay more than about ten seconds. Repeat the command to stay as often as necessary. Then release the dog with an "Okay!" And be sure to praise him for a job well done.

In the following lessons, you can increase the time of the stay until the dog will hold the sit for at least three minutes. When your dog is able to do this, you are ready to go on to the stand-stay.

Stand-Stay: This command teaches your dog to stand in place. It may not seem very important, but it can be a big help when you need to comb and brush him.

Start by teaching this command while your dog is heeling. As you slow down, say, "Stand!" and pull back on the leash. At the same time, put your left hand in front of the upper part of the dog's right hind leg. This will keep him from sitting, which he will start to do. If he does sit, don't scold him. He's only doing what he has already learned. Just start again. When you have him standing, continue to say, "Stand!" Then tell him, "Stay!"

Practice the heel and sit and the heel and stand. He'll learn to listen for a command and, if there is no command, to sit.

You can now teach the stand-stay. With the dog in the stand position, hold your hand in front of his nose and say, "Stay!" Then, holding the leash, take a step away. If the dog starts to move, say, "No, stay!" Slowly increase the time until he can hold the stand-stay for one minute as you move around him.

When he has learned this lesson, you can begin the down lesson.

Down: On this command, your dog should lie down instantly. He should do this at any time and from any position, even when he is running.

Give the dog the command to sit. Then kneel down beside him. Reach your left arm over his shoulder and grasp his left front leg. Take his right front leg in your right hand. Give the command, "Down!" As you do so, gently lift his front legs and slide him into the down position. Then put your left hand on his back to hold him down, or pull down on the leash with your left hand in order to make him stay down. Keep saying "Down! Stay!" After a few seconds, release him and praise him.

Give the dog the command to sit, and go through the down lesson again. Repeat this until the dog goes down and stays down on command, without any help.

Next, practice the down-stay on a long leash. When the dog will go down and stay while you walk away from him or walk around him, you can move on to the most important lesson of all—the come.

Come: At the command, "Come!" your dog should come to you at once and sit down facing you. Although come is the most important of the six basic commands, it should be taught last. Your dog is now used to obeying commands, to doing what *you* want, all of which will make it easier to teach him to come.

Walk forward, with the dog at heel. Stop suddenly, take a step backward, and say, "Rex, come!" As you say this, give the leash a tug to turn the dog toward you. When he is turned around, start walking backwards. Keep repeating, "Come! Good boy! Come!" as you gently tug the leash.

When he is moving at a good pace, stop. As soon as he reaches you, say, "Sit!" If necessary, guide him into a sitting position facing you. Praise him and you are ready to begin the lesson again. Work with the dog until all you have to do is take a step backward and say, "Come!" to get him to come to you and sit. Next, sit the dog a leash-length away and say, "Come!" If necessary, give the leash a slight tug.

Your dog has now mastered all of the six basic commands on the leash and is ready to work without a leash.

Going to the vet

"Vet" is short for veterinarian. A veterinarian is an animal doctor.

Take your new puppy to the vet as soon as possible. The pup will need shots to protect it against distemper, rabies, and other doggy ills. It will also need medicine for worms. The vet will show you how to give the medicine to your puppy.

You should take your dog to the vet for regular checkups and shots. In most places, the law says that your dog must have booster shots each year for rabies and other diseases. The vet will give you a tag to put on your dog's collar to show that this has been done. When necessary, the vet will clip your dog's toenails and clean its teeth.

Watch your dog to see how it acts when it is healthy. Then you'll know when something might be wrong. A change may mean nothing, but if it continues you should check with the vet. Next to you, the vet is your dog's best friend.

When you get a puppy, have its health checked at once. A veterinarian is giving this sad-eyed pup a complete physical examination.

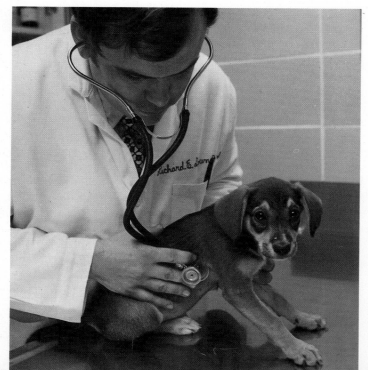

Traveling with your dog

If you take your dog along on vacation trips, don't forget about his comfort and safety. This boy takes advantage of a stop to lead his Rottweiler from its travel cage so that it can have a short walk.

What should you do with your dog when you go on vacation? If you don't take the dog, it's best to put him in a boarding kennel. But what if you want to take your dog with you?

First, check with the places where you plan to stay. Dogs may not be welcome. If you're going by car, get a folding wire cage for the dog. It will keep the dog from hopping around in the car and from jumping out when a door is opened. And never leave your dog in the car with the windows closed. In hot weather, a dog can die very quickly in a closed car.

When making a stop, give the dog water and take him for a walk. Put the leash on *before* you open the door—and keep it on. If your dog gets loose, he might get lost. Just in case, put a special identification tag on your dog's collar. Remember, your home address and phone number won't help if you are away from home.

If you're going by train or plane, you will have to make special arrangements for shipping the dog. Dogs must usually travel in special crates, in the baggage car or compartment. So check well in advance with the railroad or the airline to find out what you have to do.

Little dog lost

Look at the little dog! It has been running and searching for hours. It sniffs at everyone, hoping to find its owner. It darts across a crowded street. Horns honk. Brakes screech. The dog is tired, frightened, and thirsty. A police car zooms to the curb. A friendly voice calls to the dog—the first friendly voice the dog has heard in hours.

Luckily, the little dog is wearing tags. One tag shows that the dog has had its yearly rabies shot. Another tag is the dog's license. And there is still another tag with the owner's name, address, and phone number. The policeman phones the owner, who comes to the police station to claim the dog. The little dog is lost no longer!

Not all stray dogs are so lucky. Many strays are killed by cars. Others, without tags, are picked up and brought to a pound. A pound is a place where stray animals are kept for a short time. If nobody claims the animal, it may be sold. But if nobody buys it, it is killed.

Don't let this happen to your dog. Try to see that your dog doesn't run loose. Walk your dog on a leash. At home, keep your dog in a fenced-in dog run, or on a long chain attached to a stake or overhead wire. See that your dog always wears its collar and tags. Then, anyone who finds your dog will be able to find you. If your dog is ever missing, call your local police department, the dog shelters in your area, and the dog pound.

Of course, there will be times when your dog does get loose. And there will be times when you will let your dog run free. But if you've trained your dog well, he'll come back when you call him. That's what obedience training is all about.

Together again! This lucky Dalmatian is lost no longer.

A letter to *my* best friend

Dear friend,

I'm the puppy that's waiting for you. I'll know you right away. When you reach down to pet me, I'll wag my tail and lick your hand. For me, it will be love at first sight. I'll always be *your* best friend. But will you be *my* best friend? Will you remember that I'm a play*mate*, not a play*thing?*

I have a lot to learn, and you're going to have to teach me. You will have to feed me, make sure I always have a bowl of fresh water, and walk me when I need to go out.

You will have to be patient with me when I make mistakes. Like people, puppies often make mistakes. Like you, I can get sick. Then, I'll need the help of a dog doctor. And will you make sure I'm taken care of whenever you go away?

There are lots of responsibilities when you have a dog. Sometimes, people decide that a dog is just too much trouble. Then they give the dog to an animal shelter. Most of these dogs end up being put to death. Other people sometimes leave unwanted dogs in the woods or along a highway. If the dogs aren't killed by cars, they may starve to death. Even worse, some return to the wild and run in packs. Then the dogs may hurt people. Many abandoned dogs end up in the dog pound, where most of them are put to death.

If you take me, please have me operated on so I won't have any puppies. I won't mind. There are too many dogs in the world now. Many will never find a home or know a friend. I wouldn't want that to happen to any puppies of mine.

I'll need shots each year. And I'll need a license. Finally, to help me if I'm ever lost, please get a tag with your name, address, and telephone number on it and attach it to my collar.

So, if you're ready, so am I. We've got a lot of living and happy times to share. I'll always be there when you need me. I'll protect you and love you for the rest of my life.

I'll be *your* best friend and I want you to be *my* best friend. Please come and get me. I'm waiting for you!

Your puppy

Be your dog's best friend. If you love your pal, don't let him run loose. Stray dogs may bite people, be hit by cars, or be put to death in the dog pound.

271

If I had a hundred dollars to spend,
  Or maybe a little more,
I'd hurry as fast as my legs would go
  Straight to the animal store.

I wouldn't say, "How much for this or that?"—
  "What kind of dog is he?"
I'd buy as many as rolled an eye,
  Or wagged a tail at me!

I'd take the hound with the drooping ears
  That sits by himself alone;
Cockers and Cairns and wobbly pups
  For to be my very own.

from *The Animal Store*
Rachel Field

9

Dogs to know

Dogs to know

What kind of dog do you like best? If you like purebred dogs, there are many different kinds. There are big dogs and little dogs, indoor dogs and outdoor dogs, dogs with long hair and dogs with short hair. So take your pick!

There are 129 breeds shown and described here and on the following pages. These include the 122 breeds registered by the American Kennel Club (AKC) as well as the seven breeds the AKC now admits to the Miscellaneous Class. Most of these breeds are recognized by kennel clubs in other countries.

The dogs are drawn to scale, and shown as they appear when full-grown. This way, you can see how big—or how small—one dog is compared to another. All told, 141 dogs are pictured. This is so you can see some of the varieties in a few of the breeds. For example, there are six different kinds of Dachshund! You can get a Shorthaired, a Longhaired, or a Wirehaired Dachshund. Each comes in two sizes, Standard and Miniature! And each also comes in a number of different colors!

The short paragraph under each picture tells you some of the things you might want to know about the breed. At the end of the paragraph you will find the group to which the AKC assigns the breed. There are six such groups: Sporting Dogs, Hounds, Working Dogs, Terriers, Toys, and Nonsporting Dogs. In addition, there is a Miscellaneous Class for breeds to which the AKC grants some recognition but does not yet admit to registration in the Stud Book.

Many of the breeds shown here, as well as other breeds, appear elsewhere in this book. So, if you want more information, turn to the Index.

Afghan Hound (AF guhn) gets its name from the country of Afghanistan, where it was once a royal hunting dog. This large, swift, high-leaping hound hunts by sight. Although proud-looking, the Afghan loves to play. Its long, silky coat needs lots of care. [Hound Group]

Airedale Terrier is the largest dog in the Terrier Group. This wiry-coated dog is named for the Aire Valley in northern England. Absolutely fearless, the Airedale is also loving and gentle. [Terrier Group]

Akita (ah KEE tah) is a strong dog with a short, rough coat and a curly tail. The breed comes from Japan, where it is a national monument. Bred as a hunter, the Akita is now used as a police and guard dog. It is also a faithful family dog. [Working Group]

Affenpinscher (AH fuhn pihn shuhr) is a small, lively bundle of energy. It has a stiff, wiry, shaggy coat. Its German name means "monkey terrier." The Affenpinscher is a playful pet and a fine house dog. [Toy Group]

Alaskan Malamute (MAH luh myoot) is a native Alaskan Dog. It is named for the Malemiut Eskimos, who bred it as a sled dog. A strong, rugged animal, the Malamute has a thick, heavy coat and really enjoys the coldest weather. This friendly, lovable dog also makes an excellent pet. [Working Group]

American Water Spaniel is a fine, all-around shooting dog. Its thick, curly coat protects it from cold water and thorny bushes. Eager to please, it both flushes and retrieves. *See also* Irish Water Spaniel. [Sporting Group]

American Foxhound was bred to hunt foxes and is not often kept as a pet. Strong and fast, it hunts by scent and can stay on the trail for hours. When a foxhound gives tongue, its deep bay can be heard over great distances. These dogs are trained to hunt alone or in packs. *See also* English Foxhound. [Hound Group]

Australian Cattle Dog was bred in Australia. Now popular there as a show dog, it is still widely used to herd cattle. A fast, smart worker, it is also a fine pet and very good with children. [Miscellaneous Class]

Australian Kelpie is a smart, alert sheep dog that was first bred in Australia. It is named for a water spirit in Scottish folklore. The Kelpie's nature is such that the dog needs to be kept active and busy. [Miscellaneous Class]

American Staffordshire Terrier was first bred in the United States for pit fighting. It has a short, stiff coat, is a fine pet, and a good watchdog. These dogs are unusual because if sold or given away they accept a new master fairly quickly. *See also* Staffordshire Bull Terrier. [Terrier Group]

Australian Terrier was bred to hunt rodents and other small animals, but is now mostly a pet. It has a harsh, straight coat and a soft-haired topknot. An ideal housedog, it is very patient with children. [Terrier Group]

275

Basenji (buh SEHN jee) is a hunting dog that comes from central Africa. This dog does not bark, but makes a whining sound when happy. It has a short, silky coat. The Basenji is very intelligent and loves to play. [Hound Group]

Bedlington Terrier is a dog that looks like a lamb, but has the heart of a lion. Its soft, fleecy coat should be kept trimmed. Most owners soon learn how to do this. The breed is named for Bedlington, England, where it was first bred. This terrier may tend to be rather cranky and snappy. [Terrier Group]

Basset Hound is a short-legged, short-haired hunting dog with a long, heavy body and a sad-looking face. Its name comes from the French word *bas*, meaning "low." The friendly Basset is a good family dog. [Hound Group]

Beagle is a small hunting dog with a smooth coat. A favorite for hunting rabbits, this dog will work alone or in a pack. The gentle, affectionate Beagle is a good dog for the country or the city. [Hound Group]

Belgian Malinois (mal uh NWAH) is named after the town in Belgium where it was first bred. It has a short, fawn-colored coat and is often mistaken for the kind of dog that is called a German Shepherd. Very intelligent and alert, the Malinois is a good watchdog, but may be difficult to handle. [Working Group]

Bearded Collie is named for the hairs around its muzzle. Unlike other collies, the Bearded Collie has a harsh, shaggy coat and a blunt head. The Bearded Collie is a fine sheep dog and a good family pet. [Working Group]

Belgian Sheepdog is closely related to the Malinois, but its coat is long and black. At one time, this dog, the Malinois, and a dog called the Tervuren, were all called Belgian Sheepdogs. Now, only the black-haired dog is known by this name. A willing worker, it is often used for police work. [Working Group]

Belgian Tervuren (TUR vurn) is closely related to the Malinois and the Belgian Sheepdog. It has a long coat of fawn- or mahogany-colored, black-tipped hair. Named for the town of Tervuren, Belgium, the Tervuren was bred as a sheep dog. Like most sheep dogs, it is alert, intelligent, and loyal. This dog has scored well in obedience trials. [Working Group]

Black and Tan Coonhound is the only kind of coonhound recognized by the AKC as purebred. This dog hunts by scent. Its specialty is the raccoon, but it is also used to hunt larger animals. It has a short, thick coat that is black and tan. [Hound Group]

Bernese Mountain Dog takes its name from the Canton of Bern, Switzerland. The ancestors of these dogs were brought into Switzerland by Roman soldiers more than two thousand years ago. The basket weavers of Bern once used these dogs to pull small wagons. The Bernese is a loyal one-person dog. Its long, wavy coat does not need much grooming. [Working Group]

Bloodhound is a dog famous for its ability to follow a scent. Often used to find lost people, the gentle Bloodhound will not attack a person. A loving dog, it makes an excellent pet. Its name is short for "blooded hound." *Blooded* is a term used for an animal that comes from good stock. [Hound Group]

Bichon Frise (BEE shahn free ZAY) is a very lively little dog whose French name means "curly little dear." And the curly haired Bichon has been a "little dear," or lap dog, for hundreds of years. Sailors of long ago traded these sturdy, smart dogs in ports all around the world. The Bichon's thick, loose curls need grooming. [Nonsporting Group]

Border Collie is a dog that has helped to herd sheep in all parts of the world. Also known as the Farm Collie or Working Collie, it is one of the finest of all sheep dogs. The Border Collie is an alert watchdog, makes a fine pet, and is good with children. [Miscellaneous Class]

Border Terrier is an old English breed that comes from the border country of northern England. A small hunting dog, it is now bred mainly as a family pet. [Terrier Group]

Borzoi (BAWR zoy) is a tall, lean hunting dog with a long, silky coat. This dog used to be called a Russian Wolfhound. The name *Borzoi* is Russian for "swift." [Hound Group]

Boston Terrier was first bred in Boston about a hundred years ago. It is part English Bulldog and part terrier. Gentle, smart, and courageous, the Boston likes people and is a favorite family pet. [Nonsporting Group]

Bouvier des Flandres (boo VYAY day FLAHN druh) has a rough, wiry coat. Its name means "cowherd of Flanders." It is a good herder and watchdog. [Working Group]

Boxer is a strong, stocky dog with a short, shiny coat. Playful and patient with children, it makes a good family pet. It is also often used for police work and as a guide dog for the blind. No one is sure how the Boxer got its name, but it may be from the way it uses its front paws in a fight. [Working Group]

Briard (bree AHRD) comes from France and is named for its home, the district of Brie. This dog has a heavy, shaggy coat and likes to be outdoors. It is often used on farms and ranches to help herd cattle and sheep. Fearless and faithful, the Briard is an excellent watchdog. [Working Group]

Brittany Spaniel is named for the province of Brittany, in France. A popular hunting dog, it is the only spaniel that uses its nose to point at game. The Brittany Spaniel has a short, thick coat. Many of these dogs are born without tails, or with only short stubs. The Brittany is a good pet. [Sporting Group]

Brussels Griffon is a small dog with lots of charm and an amusing expression. There are two types of coat—rough and smooth. Although very bright, the Griffon is often hard to train to the leash. [Toy Group]

Bulldog is the national dog of Great Britian and the mascot of the British Navy. This dog is short and heavy, with a smooth coat. In spite of its looks, the Bulldog is very gentle and loves children. [Nonsporting Group]

Bullmastiff is a cross between the Mastiff and the Bulldog. It is a big, strong dog with a short, heavy coat. Fearless, alert, and obedient, the Bullmastiff makes a good family watchdog. [Working Group]

Bull Terrier comes in two varieties—white and colored. Bred as a fighting dog, the Bull Terrier sometimes needs a firm hand. But this dog has an even temper, is a fine companion, and very good with children. [Terrier Group]

Cairn Terrier is a small dog with a hard, shaggy coat. Its name came from its ability to go after small animals in heaps of stones called cairns. Easy to care for, the Cairn is at home anywhere. [Terrier Group]

Cardigan Welsh Corgi (KAWR ghee) has a dense, medium-length coat and a tail like a fox. The name *Corgi* means "dwarf dog." A herd dog, the Corgi is also a good house dog. *See also* Pembroke Welsh Corgi. [Working Group]

Cavalier King Charles Spaniel is a Toy dog with long, shaggy ears and feathery fur on its chest and legs. Although lively, it does not need much exercise. It makes a good pet for apartment dwellers. [Miscellaneous Class]

Chesapeake Bay Retriever is a·hunting dog with a short, thick coat. This dog can work in cold, rough water for a long time. Many people think it is the best of all the retrievers. The Chesapeake was named for the area in which it was first bred. [Sporting Group]

Chihuahua (chee WAH wah) is the smallest breed of dog. There are two types, one with a smooth coat and one with a long coat. A good dog for a small apartment, the Chihuahua is curious, mischievous, and alert. [Toy Group]

Chow Chow, usually called just Chow, comes from China. It is the only breed of dog that has a blue-black tongue. A one-person dog, the Chow Chow may sometimes be short-tempered with children. [Nonsporting Group]

Clumber Spaniel gets its name from an English country estate, Clumber Park. The largest and heaviest of the land spaniels, the Clumber has a silky white coat with orange or lemon-colored markings. [Sporting Group]

Cocker Spaniel has a soft, thick coat. The smallest of the Sporting Dogs, it is also known as the American Cocker. Gentle and playful, the Cocker is a very popular dog, loves children, and is more likely to be kept as a pet than used for hunting. [Sporting Group]

Collie was first bred in Scotland to herd sheep. There are two types, the familiar Rough Collie and the seldom-seen Smooth Collie. The dogs are alike except for their coats. *See also* Bearded Collie; Border Collie. [Working Group]

Coonhound, *see* Black and Tan Coonhound

Corgi, *see* Cardigan Welsh Corgi; Pembroke Welsh Corgi

Curly-Coated Retriever is named for its tight, curly coat, which usually requires a fair amount of grooming. This dog is active and loves to swim. Faithful and intelligent, it is easily trained, a good hunting dog, and a wonderful companion. [Sporting Group]

Dachshund (DAHKS hund) comes from Germany. Its name means "badger hound." There are three varieties—Smooth, Longhaired, and Wirehaired. All three kinds come in two sizes—Standard and Miniature. Lively and fun-loving, the Dachshund is a popular pet and a good dog for apartment dwellers. [Hound Group]

Dalmatian (dal MAY shun) is named for the district of Dalmatia, in Yugoslavia. Hardy and clean, the Dalmatian is a good family pet and a fine watchdog. [Nonsporting Group]

Dandie Dinmont Terrier is named for a farmer in a book by Sir Walter Scott. This playful dog has a shaggy coat and hind legs that are longer than its front legs. [Terrier Group]

Doberman Pinscher (DOH buhr muhn PIHN shuhr) is a short-haired dog that was bred in Germany for police work. The Doberman is fearless, alert, and obedient. [Working Group]

English Cocker Spaniel is bigger than its American cousin. Intelligent and willing, the English Cocker is a good hunter and a merry family dog. [Sporting Group]

English Foxhound is one of the oldest breeds of hound. Trained to hunt in packs, these dogs are sturdy and heavy boned, with straight legs and short, dense coats. Because most foxhounds would rather hunt than be around people, very few of these dogs are kept as pets. *See also* American Foxhound. [Hound Group]

English Setter is thought by many people to be one of the most beautiful of all dogs. It has a medium-length, flat coat, and a straight, well-feathered tail. It is a born hunter, and is better suited to the country than the city. Graceful, proud, and gentle, the English Setter is a one-person dog. [Sporting Group]

English Springer Spaniel got its name from the way it hunts—it makes the game "spring" from its hiding place. Friendly and smart, the English Springer is a popular hunting dog that works well on land and in water. It is a good retriever. [Sporting Group]

English Toy Spaniel has a long, silky coat. There are two varieties—solid color and broken color. These little dogs have long been a favorite of English royalty. [Toy Group]

Field Spaniel is a hunting dog with a flat, shiny coat, usually black. Intelligent and obedient, this hard-working spaniel retrieves well on land or in water. [Sporting Group]

Flat-Coated Retriever has a dense, sleek coat, usually black or liver-colored. A good hunter and companion, this dog is a strong swimmer and loves water. [Sporting Group]

Foxhound, *see* American Foxhound; English Foxhound

Fox Terrier can have a smooth or wiry coat. It was first bred in England to go after foxes in their dens. Gay, mischievous, and playful, this dog is a popular pet in city or country. [Terrier Group]

French Bulldog has a smooth coat, batlike ears, a typical bulldog face, and a short tail. Playful and curious, it is easily housebroken. A good watchdog, as well as a good playmate for children, this dog is ideal for apartment dwellers. [Nonsporting Group]

German Shepherd Dog, called an Alsatian in Great Britain, was first bred in Germany as a herd dog. Later, it was used as a war dog. Today, this very intelligent dog is used for police work, as a guard dog, a guide dog for the blind, and has even taken over from the Saint Bernard as a rescue dog in the Alps. A loyal family dog, the German Sheperd is very good with children. [Working Group]

German Shorthaired Pointer is a hunting dog with a short, hard coat. Although it works more slowly than setters or other pointers, the Shorthair is a good, all-around gundog that can hunt and retrieve almost any kind of game in field or water. [Sporting Group]

German Wirehaired Pointer has a dense, soft undercoat and a rough, wiry outercoat that gives it good protection in rough brush or cold water. This all-purpose hunter, developed in Germany, works well on land or in water and is a good retriever. [Sporting Group]

Gordon Setter was named after a Scottish nobleman. Its long, soft coat may be flat or slightly waved. Like other setters, it marks game by pointing with its nose. A fine pet, it is gentle with children. [Sporting Group]

Giant Schnauzer (SHNOW zuhr) was developed in Germany to help drive cattle to market. Its name means "snout" or "muzzle." This dog has a shaggy muzzle and shaggy eyebrows. It is a loyal family dog. *See also* Miniature Schnauzer; Standard Schnauzer. [Working Group]

Great Dane is a giant dog that needs lots of space. In spite of its name it was bred in Germany, not Denmark. Its coat may be any of five colors. A Dane with black patches is called a Harlequin. [Working Group]

Golden Retriever has a thick, flat or wavy double coat and lots of feathering. First bred in Scotland, the self-confident Golden is eager to please and easy to train. A fine field or water dog, the Golden is also an excellent family dog. [Sporting Group]

Great Pyrenees (PIHR uh neez) is a large dog with a long, flat, heavy coat. It was named for the mountains between France and Spain, where it was used to herd sheep. The Pyrenees is a good dog around children. [Working Group]

Greyhound was known in Egypt more than three thousand years ago. It hunts by sight and is the fastest of all dogs. The Greyhound is best known as a racing dog. [Hound Group]

Griffon, *see* Brussels Griffon; Wirehaired Pointing Griffon

Irish Setter has a silky, dark-red coat. Bred in Ireland, this hunting dog is spirited, gentle, and lovable. Many of the first Irish Setters were white with red markings. Today, the ones seen most often are a rich mahogany color. Although a good gundog, this setter is more popular as a pet. [Sporting Group]

Harrier (HAR ee uhr) has a short, flat coat and looks like a small English Foxhound. It hunts by scent and was bred to chase hares, which are large relatives of the rabbit. Harriers usually hunt in packs. [Hound Group]

Husky, *see* Siberian Husky

Irish Terrier, one of the oldest of all the terrier breeds, does not look like any other terrier. It has a hard, wiry, medium-length coat. Fearless and bold, the Irish Terrier has been used to hunt lions. At home in the city or country, this dog is a fine companion for a child. [Terrier Group]

Ibizan Hound (ee BEE sahn) comes from the island of Ibiza in the Mediterranean Sea. There are three types of coat—smooth, wire, and long. This dog hunts by scent, points, and retrieves. [Miscellaneous Group]

Irish Water Spaniel has a curly coat, a topknot on its head, and a so-called "rat tail." This hunting dog is a strong swimmer, works best in water, and is particularly good at retrieving ducks and other water birds. *See also* American Water Spaniel. [Sporting Group]

Kerry Blue Terrier has a soft, dense, wavy coat that is blue-gray in color. The Kerry Blue comes from County Kerry, in Ireland, for which it is named. Known in Ireland as the Irish Blue, it is a good hunter, herder, and also a fine companion. [Terrier Group]

Irish Wolfhound, the tallest of all dogs, has a rough, wiry coat. Though bred to hunt wolves, this hound is one of the gentlest of all breeds. It is dignified and quiet, but needs plenty of room. [Hound Group]

Italian Greyhound looks like a miniature Greyhound. This dog has been a popular pet since Roman times. It has large, expressive eyes and a short, sleek coat. [Toy Group]

Japanese Spaniel has a silky, feathery coat. There are several types and colors, but most Japanese Spaniels are black and white. This dog's original home was China. [Toy Group]

Komondor (KOH mahn dawr) is a shepherd dog from Hungary. Its thick, white coat makes it look as if it is covered with long cords. One of the oldest breeds in Europe, the Komondor is a good guard dog but may be a difficult pet to handle. [Working Group]

Keeshond (KAYS hahnd), the national dog of The Netherlands, is named after a famous Dutch patriot. This dog has a thick, straight coat and is a fine companion. [Nonsporting Group]

Kuvasz (KOO vahz) is a large, strong dog. Its ancestors came from Tibet, but the breed was developed in Hungary. Its name comes from a Turkish word that means "armed guard of the nobility." The Kuvasz requires an experienced owner who knows dogs. [Working Group]

285

Labrador Retriever, perhaps the most popular retriever, is also a fine family dog. In spite of its name, it comes from Newfoundland, not Labrador. Its coat may be black, yellow, or chocolate in color. [Sporting Group]

Lakeland Terrier was first bred in the Lake District of northern England, where it was used to hunt foxes and otters. Bold but friendly, the small, sturdy Lakeland is a good family dog. [Terrier Group]

Lhasa Apso (LAH suh AP soh) has a long, heavy coat that needs lots of grooming. Originally from Lhasa, the capital of Tibet, it is known as the "lion dog." In Tibet, this dog is an indoor watchdog. [Nonsporting Group]

Malamute, *see* Alaskan Malamute

Maltese was probably developed on the island of Malta more than two thousand years ago. This spirited little animal may have been the first lap dog. It has a long, silky, white coat that needs care. [Toy Group]

Manchester Terrier is a breed that comes in two varieties, Toy and Standard. Named for Manchester, England, these dogs are very clean house dogs. [Terrier Group and Toy Group]

Mastiff, or **Old English Mastiff**, is a giant dog with a short coat. Although bred long ago as a fighting dog, the Mastiff is good-natured. It makes a fine family dog for people who like really big dogs. [Working Group]

Miniature Bull Terrier is a small dog that is slowly gaining in popularity. It is a variety of the larger Bull Terrier. The two dogs differ only in size and weight. [Miscellaneous Class]

Miniature Pinscher (PIN shuhr) is a small dog with a short, smooth coat. It looks like a small Doberman Pinscher, but is an older breed. Proud and peppy, it makes a playful pet and a good watchdog. [Toy Group]

Miniature Schnauzer (SHNOW zuhr) has a thick, wiry coat. A very popular dog, it is alert, active, and fond of children. *See also* Giant Schnauzer; Standard Schnauzer. [Terrier Group]

Newfoundland is a huge dog with a long, full coat. Long known as a playmate and protector of children, this strong, fearless dog loves the water and has gained a reputation for rescuing drowning people. [Working Group]

Norwegian Elkhound has a thick, gray coat. This dog was bred in Norway about three thousand years ago to hunt elk. It has lots of energy, is very clean, and is a loyal family dog. [Hound Group]

Norwich Terrier is named for Norwich, England. There are two types—drop ear and prick ear. The Norwich has a hard, wiry coat and is an ideal house dog. [Terrier Group]

Old English Sheepdog has a heavy, shaggy coat that should be brushed regularly. This dog walks like a shuffling bear. Many inexperienced owners have found the Old English Sheepdog a difficult animal to handle. [Working Group]

Otter Hound, bred in England to hunt otters, has a rough, thick coat. This hound is a fine swimmer and can work in cold water for long periods of time. [Hound Group]

Papillon (PAH pee yohn) has long silky hair and a bushy tail. Its name is the French word for "butterfly," and its ears do look a bit like a butterfly's wings. Dainty and lively, this dog is a loving pet. [Toy Group]

Pekingese (pee kihng EEZ) was once the royal dog of China. It has only been known outside China for about a hundred years. Stubborn and independent, but playful and loyal, the little Peke is a good family pet. [Toy Group]

Pembroke Welsh Corgi (KAWR gee) has a dense, medium-length coat and a short tail. The name *Corgi* is from two Welsh words meaning "dwarf dog." The Pembroke is a good house dog. *See also* Cardigan Welsh Corgi. [Working Group]

Pointer is a very popular gundog. It has a short coat and houndlike ears, head, and body. It "points" birds with one front paw lifted and its tail stiff. *See also* German Shorthaired Pointer; German Wirehaired Pointer; Spinoni Italiani; Vizsla. [Sporting Group]

Pomeranian is a small dog with a thick, fluffy coat. It is related to the strong sled dogs of Iceland and Lapland. Smart, lively, and even-tempered, the Pomeranian makes a good watchdog because of its sharp bark. [Toy Group]

Poodle is a very intelligent and popular dog. For shows, its thick, curly coat is clipped in one of the styles shown. There are three varieties of Poodle—Standard, Miniature, and Toy. [Nonsporting Group and Toy Group]

Pug, the largest dog in the Toy Group, has a soft, short coat, a black muzzle, and a tightly curled tail. The Pug was probably bred in China and brought to Europe by the Dutch. For many years, it was a favorite in the Dutch and English royal courts. Alert and clean, the Pug requires little care. [Toy Group]

Puli (POO lee) is a medium-sized dog that has long been used by the shepherds of Hungary. The Puli often controls a runaway sheep by jumping on its back and riding it until it tires out! Alert and active, the Puli is good guard dog. Its thick, shaggy coat tends to make the Puli look larger than it is. [Working Group]

Retriever, *see* Chesapeake Bay Retriever; Curly-Coated Retriever; Flat-Coated Retriever; Golden Retriever; Labrador Retriever

Rhodesian Ridgeback, or African Lion Hound, is a brave, swift hound with a short, sleek coat. A ridge of hair on its back that grows in the opposite direction to the rest of its coat gives this dog its name. Well-behaved, quiet, and easily trained, the Rhodesian is suited to country or city life. [Hound Group]

Rottweiler (RAHT wy luhr), named after the village in Germany where it was first bred, is descended from Roman cattle dogs. This dog's hair is short, coarse, and flat. The strong, brave, and calm Rottweiler is a fine companion and guard dog. [Working Group]

Saint Bernard is very famous for finding lost travelers in the snowy Swiss Alps. In addition to the familiar short-haired dog, there is also a long-haired variety. Big and strong, the Saint Bernard may sometimes be rather difficult to handle. [Working Group]

Saluki (suh LOO kee), or Gazelle Hound, is thought to be the oldest purebred dog in the world. Named for an ancient Arabian city, the swift Saluki hunts by sight. The Saluki has a short, silky coat with feathering about the ears, legs, and tail. [Hound Group]

Samoyed (sam uh YEHD) comes from northern Siberia. The Samoyed people first bred this dog to guard reindeer herds and to pull sleds. Popular as a pet and watchdog, this big, white dog with the "smiling" face is a loyal and intelligent animal. [Working Group]

Schnauzer, *see* Giant Schnauzer; Miniature Schnauzer; Standard Schnauzer

Schipperke (SKIHP uhr kee) has a heavy, black coat and may be born without a tail. It comes from Belgium, and its name means "little boatman." It was once used to guard barges, and to hurry the horses that pulled barges through Belgian canals. [Nonsporting Group]

Scottish Deerhound is a very large, graceful hound with a harsh, wiry coat. First bred in Scotland as a royal hunting dog, it is now used to hunt game other than deer. A quiet dog, and easy to train, the Deerhound should have room to run. [Hound Group]

Scottish Terrier, or "Scottie" as it is often called, is a small terrier. Its hard, wiry coat looks better when trimmed. Brave and alert, the Scottie is an excellent little hunter. Very popular as a pet, it is suited to life in a house or apartment. [Terrier Group]

Sealyham Terrier is a small terrier with a wiry coat. It is named after the estate in Wales where it was first bred. The Sealyham has an even temper, is well-mannered, and a good house dog. [Terrier Group]

Setter, *see* English Setter; Gordon Setter; Irish Setter

Shetland Sheepdog comes from the Shetland Islands, near Scotland. Small and long-haired, the "Sheltie" is stronger than it looks. Bred as a herder, it likes the outdoors, but is a good house dog and pet. [Working Group]

Shih Tzu (shee dzoo) comes from Tibet and China. Its name, which is Chinese, means "lion's son." Courageous and hardy, this little dog is always playful. Its long, dense coat may be any color. [Toy Group]

Siberian Husky was bred in the Arctic as a sled dog, but it can live anywhere. Naturally friendly, gentle, and clean, the Siberian is a good pet and companion. It is at home in the city or the country. [Working Group]

Silky Terrier is an Australian dog. It has a long, silky coat and is related to the Australian and Yorkshire terriers. Friendly and curious, the Silky Terrier is an ideal house dog where space is limited. [Toy Group]

Skye Terrier, one of the oldest of the many terrier breeds, comes from the Scottish island of Skye. This dog has a long, flowing coat that needs grooming. A bold hunter, the Skye is also a good watchdog. [Terrier Group]

Soft-Coated Wheaten Terrier comes from Ireland. It has a shaggy coat of soft, wavy fur. The puppies have dark coats that turn the color of wheat in about two years. The Wheaten likes children and is easily trained. [Terrier Group]

Spaniel, *see* American Water Spaniel; Brittany Spaniel; Cavalier King Charles Spaniel; Clumber Spaniel; Cocker Spaniel; English Cocker Spaniel; English Springer Spaniel; English Toy Spaniel; Field Spaniel; Irish Water Spaniel; Japanese Spaniel; Sussex Spaniel; Welsh Springer Spaniel

Spinoni Italiani (spee NOH nee ih tahl YAH nee), or Italian Griffon, is a coarse-haired pointer. This all-purpose gundog, long a favorite in Italy, is slowly becoming better known in other lands. [Miscellaneous Class]

Sussex Spaniel is named for the county of Sussex in southern England, where this dog was first bred. The Sussex is a strong, stocky dog, with short legs and a flat or slightly wavy coat. Unlike other spaniels, the Sussex often barks while it is hunting. It is a good, dependable gundog, makes a fine pet, and is excellent with children. [Sporting Group]

Staffordshire Bull Terrier has a short, smooth coat. First bred in Staffordshire, England, as a fighting dog, it is fearless, obedient, and good-tempered. The Staffordshire is a fine family pet and gentle with children. *See also* American Staffordshire Terrier. [Terrier Group]

Tibetan Terrier, which is not a true terrier, was bred by Buddhist monks in the mountains of Tibet. It has a thick, shaggy coat and a fluffy tail that curls over its back. Most Tibetans once believed that this dog would bring good luck to its owner. An active dog, the Tibetan enjoys both hot and cold weather. It makes an excellent family pet and is a loving companion. [Nonsporting Group]

Standard Schnauzer (SHNOW zuhr) is the oldest of the three Schnauzer breeds. Like the others, it has a thick, wiry coat, a beard, a bushy eyebrows. First known as a Wirehaired Pinscher, it takes its present name from a winning dog named Schnauzer. *See also* Giant Schnauzer; Miniature Schnauzer. [Working Group]

Vizsla (VEEZ lah) is a medium-sized hunting dog with a short, smooth, rusty-gold coat. Also known as the Hungarian Pointer and Yellow Pointer, the Vizsla is named for a village in Hungary. A close-working gundog, the Vizsla hunts and tracks hare, points and retrieves game birds on land, and is also an excellent retriever in water. [Sporting Group]

291

Weimaraner (VY muh rah nuhr), a hunting dog from Weimar, Germany, has a sleek, gray coat. Nicknamed the "gray ghost," the Weimaraner moves smoothly in the field. This extremely intelligent dog has done exceptionally well in obedience trails. It also is a dog that loves to be part of the family. [Sporting Group]

Welsh Corgi, *see* Cardigan Welsh Corgi; Pembroke Welsh Corgi

Welsh Springer Spaniel is a very old breed of spaniel from Wales. It has a thick, silky, red-and-white coat that's straight or flat. The Welsh Springer is a fine hunter and retriever that will work in the worst weather. Gentle with children, it is a good family dog in town or country. [Sporting Group]

Welsh Terrier is a small black-and-tan terrier from Wales. This dog has a wiry coat and looks like a small Airedale. A lively hunting dog, the Welsh Terrier is also a quiet, well-mannered house dog that makes an excellent family pet and companion. [Terrier Group]

West Highland White Terrier hails from the highlands of Scotland. It has a straight, tough coat that is easy to clean with a brush. A hardy outdoor dog, the Westie is also a good house pet. [Terrier Group]

Whippet is a small racing hound with a smooth coat that's easy to groom. Speedy and graceful, the Whippet can run faster than any dog of the same weight. Quiet and dignified, it is a good family dog. [Hound Group]

Wirehaired Pointing Griffon is a hunting dog with a stiff, hard coat. A slow and careful hunter, the Wirehaired Griffon is also an excellent water dog that will work in all kinds of weather. [Sporting Group]

Yorkshire Terrier is named for Yorkshire, England. You wouldn't think so to look at this dog, but the Yorkshire was bred to catch rats. Its long, silky hair needs special grooming for show purposes. [Toy Group]

Books to read

Stories about dogs have been favorites of writers and readers down through the ages. This list is only a sampling of the many fine books about dogs. Titles marked with an asterisk (*) are available in paperback. You will find the titles of other dog books on pages 25, 103, 139, 140–141, 169, and 245. And, of course, your school or public library will have many books about dogs that you are certain to enjoy.

Ages 3 to 8

Angus and the Ducks* by Marjorie Flack
(Doubleday, 1930)
Angus, a Scotch Terrier, has some very amusing experiences when his curiosity leads him to slip through the hedge and into the garden next door. Also by the same author: *Angus and the Cat; Angus Lost.*

Benjy's Doghouse by Margaret B. Graham
(Harper & Row, 1973)
Benjy doesn't like his new doghouse, so he looks elsewhere for a place to sleep—with surprising results. Also by the same author: *Benjy and the Barking Bird.*

Bobo's Dream* by Martha Alexander
(Dial, 1970)
This wordless picture book tells of the love between a boy and his little Dachshund, Bobo. After the boy stops a large dog from stealing Bobo's bone, Bobo dreams of ways in which he saves his owner.

Finders Keepers* by William Lipkind and Nicolas Mordvinoff (Harcourt, 1951)
In this humorous story, two dogs settle a question about a bone when a third dog appears.

Go Away, Dog* by Joan L. Nodset
(Harper & Row, 1963)
A persistent puppy wins the love of a little boy who thinks he doesn't like dogs.

Harry the Dirty Dog* by Gene Zion
(Harper & Row, 1956)
Harry thinks that getting dirty is fun, but his family has other ideas. Finally, Harry begs for a hated bath in an amusing way. Also by the same author: *Harry and the Lady Next Door; Harry by the Sea; No Roses for Harry.*

Madeline's Rescue* by Ludwig Bemelmans
(Viking, 1953)
In this picture-story book in rhymed text, Madeline is rescued from the Seine River by Genevieve, a Saint Bernard. The dog is then adopted by the girls at the boarding school.

My Puppy Is Born by Joanna Cole
(Morrow, 1973)
Graphic photos and simple text show and tell about the birth of a litter of Dachshund puppies, and the first few weeks in the life of one of them.

The Nicest Gift by Leo Politi
(Scribner, 1973)
A young boy in East Los Angeles loses his dog on Christmas Eve, but the two find each other in time for a joyous Christmas.

Pantaloni by Bettina
(Harper & Row, 1957)
A small dog has some hilarious adventures when he disappears, wanders about, and finally is found in a most unexpected place.

What Mary Jo Wanted by Janice M. Udry
(Whitman, 1968)
Mary Jo wants a puppy. Her father buys her one. But when the new member of the family cries night after night, it's up to Mary Jo to find a way to keep the puppy quiet.

What Whiskers Did* by Ruth Carroll
(Walck, 1965)
This action-filled picture book without words tells the story of a runaway puppy who is helped by a rabbit family.

Whingdingdilly by Bill Peet
(Houghton Mifflin, 1970)
Scamp is a dog who wants to be a horse, but a well-meaning witch turns him into an odd mixture of animals called a Whingdingdilly.

Whistle for Willie by Ezra Jack Keats
(Viking, 1964)
A small boy has some fun when he tries to whistle for his dog the way the big boys do.

You're a Good Dog, Joe by Kurt Unkelbach
(Prentice-Hall, 1971)
The straightforward text on training a dog to obey will help a child to develop a feeling of responsibility for a pet.

Ages 9 to 12

"Banner, Forward!" The Pictorial Biography of a Guide Dog by Eva Rappaport
(Dutton, 1969)
The story of Banner, a Golden Retriever who is trained as a guide dog for the blind.

Both Ends of the Leash; Selecting and Training Your Dog* by Kurt Unkelbach
(Prentice-Hall, 1968)
The author presents his choice of the ten best breeds for children's pets.

Bringing Up Puppies; A Child's Book of Dog Breeding and Care by Jane Levin
(Harcourt, 1958)
This true story, with photographs, tells of four children who breed their Cocker Spaniel, Chip, and watch her give birth to four puppies nine weeks later. The reader learns about the care of the mother dog and the puppies.

A Dog Named Duke; True Stories of German Shepherds at Work with the Law by Leo Handel (Lippincott, 1969)
Eleven true stories, gathered from the police files of several countries, about the training of German Shepherds and how they help to track down criminals and search for stolen goods.

A Dog on Barkham Street* by Mary Stolz
(Harper & Row, 1960)
When a hobo uncle and his Collie visit Edward, the dog helps take care of the bully next door.

Dogs; Best Breeds for Young People by Wilfred S. Bronson (Harcourt, 1969)
If you're planning to buy a dog, this helpful book goes into detail about the characteristics of various breeds. The author talks of the responsibilities of owning a dog and of things seen from a dog's viewpoint.

Dominic* by William Steig
(Farrar, 1972)
Dominic, a friendly dog, sets out one day to find whatever he can. This includes new friends, a fortune, and a lifetime companion.

Go Find Hanka by Alexander Crosby
(Golden Gate Junior Books, 1970)
A bird dog is sent to find a small boy lost on the Grand Prairie of Illinois, back in the days when Abraham Lincoln was an Illinois lawyer.

Hurry Home, Candy* by Meindert DeJong
(Harper & Row, 1953)
A lost puppy is forced into the lonely life of an outcast until he finds a lasting companion in a lonely old man. Also by the same author: *Puppy Summer; Along Came a Dog; Dirk's Dog, Bello.*

The Incredible Journey by Sheila Burnford
(Little, Brown, 1961)
A Siamese cat, an old English Bull Terrier, and a Labrador Retriever find their way home through 250 miles of Canadian wilderness.

Junket; The Dog Who Liked Everything "Just So" by Anne H. White (Viking, 1955)
Life on a farm is happy for Junket, an Airedale who likes everything "just so." When the farm is sold to a man who says "no animals," Junket changes the new owner's point of view.

Kavik, the Wolf Dog* by Walter Morey
(Dutton, 1968)
After a plane crash in Alaska, teen-age Andy finds Kavik, a sled dog, nurses him back to health, and returns him to the owner. But Kavik has other ideas. Also by the same author: *Scrub Dog of Alaska.*

Kids and Dog Shows by Lynn Hall
(Follett, 1974)
Lynn Hall tells about the world of dog shows, from how to choose a dog, through getting it ready for the show, and then showing it.

The Roger Caras Pet Book by Roger Caras
(Holt, Rinehart & Winston, 1977)
This book on the joys and duties of pet owners offers sound information on more than fifty breeds of dogs, as well as other pets. A young adult book that will appeal to able readers.

Sasha, My Friend* by Barbara Corcoran
(Atheneum, 1969)
After her mother's death, young Hallie and her father move to Montana. At first, Hallie is lonely and homesick in the wilderness. But her life takes on new meaning when she finds and adopts an orphaned wolf cub.

Wild Dogs Three by Michael Fox
(Coward, 1977)
A true story of three dogs that turned wild after they were abandoned by their thoughtless owners. The book has pictures of the dogs taken over a one-year period.

New Words

Here are some of the special words and terms used by people who work with dogs. You will know some of these words because you've seen them in this book. But many of the words may be new to you. If you are interested in dogs, these are all good words to know. There are a few of these words that you may not know how to pronounce. Next to each of these, you will see how to say the word: **occiput** (AHK suh puht). The part shown in capital letters is said a little more loudly than the rest of the word.

apron: The frill of hair below the neck and on the chest of a long-haired dog such as the Collie. (See pictures, page 187.)

bat ears: Ears, such as those of the French Bulldog, that stand straight up, are wide at the base, rounded at the top, and face the front. (See picture, page 252.)

bay: The long, deep sound a hound makes when it is hunting.

beard: The very bushy whiskers on the muzzle and lower jaw of some breeds, such as the Bearded Collie. (See picture, page 276.)

bench show: A show at which dogs competing for prizes are "benched"—that is, kept on a bench before and after judging. (See picture, page 190.)

best in show: The top award at a dog show, the one given to the dog judged the best of all the dogs in the show.

best of breed: The award given at a dog show to each dog that is judged to be the best of a particular breed.

bitch: An adult female dog.

bite: The position of the upper and lower teeth when a dog's mouth is closed. *See also* **level bite, overshot, scissors bite, undershot.**

blaze: A white stripe down the middle of the face, between the eyes. (See top picture, page 11.)

breed standard: A description of the ideal dog of each recognized breed. At shows, each dog is judged by how well it matches the breed standard.

brindle (BRIHN duhl): A color of coat, caused by a mixture of light and dark hairs.

brisket: The lower part of the chest, between a dog's forelegs. (See picture, page 255.)

button ears: Ears that drop over in front to cover the ear opening. (See picture, page 45.)

canine (KAY nyn): A word that means dog or doglike. Also, any one of the group of meat-eating animals that includes dogs, foxes, wolves, coyotes, and jackals.

canines (KAY nyns): The two long, pointed teeth, or fangs, in the upper and lower jaws. The upper canine teeth are called the eyeteeth.

C.D. (Companion Dog): These initials after a dog's name mean that the dog has scored a certain number of points in novice work at American Kennel Club (AKC) obedience trials. *See also* **novice work; obedience trial.**

C.D.X. (Companion Dog Excellent): These initials after a dog's name mean that the dog has scored a certain number of points in open work at AKC obedience trials. *See also* **open work; obedience trial.**

Ch. (Champion): This abbreviation in front of a dog's name means that the dog has won a championship in competition at dog shows.

choke collar: A chain or leather collar that tightens when pulled.

dam: The female parent; the mother dog.

dewclaw: An extra claw above the paw, like a fifth toe, on the inside of the forelegs, and sometimes on the inside of the hind legs.

dock: To shorten a dog's tail by cutting part of it off. A docked tail is a standard for some breeds, such as the Doberman Pinscher. (See picture, page 281.)

dog: An adult male dog. The term is also used for all dogs, both male and female.

dual champion: A dog that has won both a show championship and a field trial championship. *See also* **Ch.; Field Ch.**

elbow: The joint between the upper arm and the forearm. (See picture, page 255.)

eyeteeth: The two long, pointed teeth (canines) in the upper jaw. *See also* **canines.**

fall: The long hair hanging down over the face of a dog such as the Skye Terrier. (See picture, page 107.)

feathering: The long fringe of hair on the ears, legs, or tail of some breeds, such as the English Setter. (See picture, page 30.)

Field Ch.: This title before a dog's name means that the dog has won its championship at field trials. *See also* **field trial.**

field trial: A contest for breeds in the Sporting Group and for some hounds. The dogs are judged by their ability and style in finding or retrieving animals, or following a scent.

flews: The loose-hanging part of the upper lip of some breeds, such as the Bulldog. (See picture, page 50.)

flush: To drive, or spring, a bird or other animal from cover, forcing it to fly or run.

gait: The way a dog walks, trots, or runs.

gay tail: A tail, such as that of the Airedale Terrier, that is carried straight up. (See picture, page 44.)

groom: To brush, comb, or trim a dog's coat.

guard hairs: The long, smooth, stiff hairs that grow through the undercoat and usually hide it.

hackles: The hair on a dog's neck and back that stands up when the dog is angry or afraid.

handler: A person who shows a dog at a dog show or works a dog at a field trial.

hard mouth: A dog that leaves teethmarks in the birds and animals it retrieves is said to have a hard mouth. This is a serious fault in a retriever. *See also* **soft mouth.**

harlequin: A coat, such as that of a Harlequin Great Dane, with odd-shaped patches of color, usually black on white. (See picture, page 283.)

heat: The time when a female is able to have puppies. This happens twice a year.

height: The height of a dog, called shoulder height, is measured from the ground to the withers. (See picture, page 255.) *See also* **withers.**

hock: The joint in a dog's hind leg. The hock is a dog's true heel. (See picture, page 255.)

hound: Any one of the dogs that hunt by sight or by scent. The Irish Wolfhound (see picture, page 37) hunts by sight. The Black and Tan Coonhound (see picture, page 36) hunts by scent.

incisors (ihn SY zuhrs): The six upper and six lower front teeth, between the canines.

kennel: A house or enclosed space where dogs are kept; also a place where dogs are bred or boarded.

Landseer: The black-and-white Newfoundlands named for Sir Edward Landseer, an English painter who often used Newfoundlands of this coloring as models. (See picture, page 41.)

leather: The loose-hanging flap of the long ears of spaniels, poodles, and some hounds. (See pictures, pages 32, 36, 50.)

length: The length of a dog's body is measured from the forechest to the back of the thigh. (See picture, page 255.)

level bite: When the upper and lower front teeth (incisors) meet edge to edge, a dog is said to have a level bite.

litter: All the puppies born at one time to a mother dog.

mask: Dark coloring, like a mask, on the front part of the head.

match show: A dog show, usually unofficial, at which no championship points are awarded.

mate: to bring a male and female together so that a litter of puppies may be born. *See also* **dog; bitch; litter.**

mixed breed: A dog whose mother or father was of two or more breeds.

mongrel: A dog whose mother and father were both mixed breeds.

muzzle: The part of the head in front of the eyes. Also, a leather strap or wire cage put on a dog's muzzle to keep the dog from biting or eating.

novice work (NAHV ihs): The obedience tests a dog must pass to earn the degree or title of Companion Dog. (*Novice* means "beginner".) *See also* **C.D.; obedience trial.**

obedience trial (oh BEE dee uhns): An event in which dogs compete to show how well they have learned to obey. Obedience degrees are earned at these trials. *See also* **C.D.; C.D.X.; U.D.**

occiput (AHK suh puht): A bony point between a dog's ears, at the upper back part of the head. (See picture, page 255.)

open work: The obedience tests a dog must pass to earn the degree or title of Companion Dog Excellent. *See also* **C.D.X.; obedience trial.**

overshot: When the upper front teeth (incisors) overlap but do not touch the lower incisors, a dog is said to have an overshot bite.

pads: The cushions, or soles, of a dog's paws. (See picture, page 255.)

pastern (PAS tuhrn): The lower part of the foreleg. (See picture, page 255.)

pedigree (PEHD uh gree): The written record of a dog's ancestors. The American Kennel Club can supply pedigrees for all registered dogs.

prick ears: Ears, such as those of the German Shepherd Dog, that stand straight up and are usually pointed. (See picture, page 173.)

puppy: Any dog less than one year old.

purebred: A dog with ancestors of the same breed.

register: To send information about your dog to an official organization such as the American Kennel Club. The organization will record the information and assign a special number to the dog.

retriever: A type of hunting dog bred and trained to retrieve (bring back) a bird or animal that has been shot. (See picture, page 195.)

ring tail: A tail, such as that of the Basenji, that curves up over the back in a circle. (See picture, page 36.)

rose ears: Ears, such as those of the Bulldog, that are folded forward with the flaps turned out, showing the inside of the ears. (See picture, page 50.)

ruff: The band of thick, long hair that grows around the neck of a dog such as a Chow Chow. (See picture, page 51.)

saber tail: A tail, such as that of the German Shepherd Dog, that hangs in a slight curve. (See picture, page 173.)

saddle: A dark marking, like a saddle, over the back. (See picture of Pointer, page 30.)

scissors bite: When the inside of the upper front teeth (incisors) touch the outside of the lower front teeth, like the blades of a scissors coming together, a dog is said to have a scissors bite.

screw tail: A naturally short tail that is twisted like a spiral.

semiprick ears: Ears, like those of the Shetland Sheepdog, that stand up, with just the tips bent forward. (See picture, page 290.)

setter: A type of dog used to find birds. A setter usually points with its nose, but it may also lift one front leg. Setters were developed from a hunting dog called a Setting Spaniel that was trained to "set" (crouch or lie down) when it found birds, so that a net could be thrown over the birds to capture them. There are three breeds of setters: English, Gordon, and Irish. (See pictures on pages 13, 30, and 254.)

sickle tail (SIHK uhl): A tail, like that of the Otter Hound, that curves out and up in a semicircle. (See picture, page 89.)

sire (syr): The male parent; the father dog.

soft mouth: A dog that retrieves birds and animals without damaging them with teethmarks is said to have a soft mouth. *See also* **hard mouth.**

spaniel (SPAN yuhl): A type of dog. The spaniel family contains more breeds than any other. The name *spaniel* comes from the word *Spain*, the country where these dogs were probably first developed.

spay: To operate on a female dog so she can't have puppies.

squirrel tail: A tail, like that of the Basset Hound, that is carried up and more or less curving forward. (See picture, page 276.)

stop: The step-up from nose to skull. Some breeds have a very sharp stop; others have a very slight stop. (See picture, page 255.)

studbook: A book containing the pedigrees and records of registered dogs. *See also* **pedigree; register.**

T.D. (Tracking Dog): These initials after a dog's name mean the dog has passed an AKC test in following a scent trail. *See also* **U.D.**

terrier: Any one of a group of dogs once bred to drive small animals out of burrows, or holes, in the ground. The name *terrier* comes from the Latin word *terra*, meaning "earth."

tulip ears: Ears that stand straight up, but with the sides curved slightly forward. The ear is shaped somewhat like a tulip petal.

U.D. (Utility Dog): These initials after a dog's name mean that the dog has scored a certain number of points in utility work at AKC obedience trials. (*Utility* means "good for all sorts of things.") This title may be combined with the title of T.D. (Tracking Dog) and shown as U.T.D. (Utility Tracking Dog). *See also* **obedience trial; T.D.; utility work.**

undershot: When the front teeth (incisors) of the lower jaw stick out beyond the front teeth of the upper jaw, a dog is said to have an undershot bite. The Bulldog has an undershot jaw.

utility work: The obedience tests a dog must pass to earn the degree or title of Utility Dog. *See also* **obedience trial; U.D.**

wean (ween): To get a puppy used to food other than its mother's milk.

whelp: A puppy that still takes milk from its mother. Also, to give birth to a litter of puppies.

whip tail: A tail such as that of the Pointer, carried straight out and stiff. (See picture, page 31.)

whiskers: Coarse hairs on the sides of the muzzle and underjaw. Whiskers are not as bushy as a beard. (See bottom picture, page 14.) *See also* **beard.**

withers: The highest point of the shoulders, just behind the neck. A dog's height (called shoulder height) is measured to the withers. (See picture, page 255.)

Illustration Acknowledgments

The publishers of *Childcraft* gratefully acknowledge the courtesy of the following photographers, agencies, and organizations for illustrations in this volume. When all the illustrations for a sequence of pages are from a single source, the inclusive page numbers are given. In all other instances, the page numbers refer to facing pages, which are considered as a single unit or spread. All illustrations are the property of the publishers of *Childcraft* unless names are marked with an asterisk (*).

Cover: Aristocrat and standard binding—Doris Pinney, Camera Clix* Heritage binding—Anubis from the tomb of Tutankhamen, Egyptian Museum, Cairo. (F. L. Kenett, © Rainbird Publishing Group, Ltd.)*; Robert H. Glaze, Artstreet*; Darrell Wiskur; Bettmann Archive*; Clyde H. Smith from Peter Arnold*; *Childcraft* photo; Sam Blakesley, Photri*; Mike Mariano; *Childcraft* photo

1–9: Jackie Geyer
10,11: J. Zimmerman, FPG*; Sam Blakesley, Photri*; Gaines Dog Research Center*; Robert H. Glaze, Artstreet*; L. Willinger, FPG*
12,13: Tana Hoban, DPI*; Judson Niver, Animals Animals from Camera Clix*; Everett C. Johnson, Photri*; John V. Dunigan, DPI*; Joanne Leonard, Woodfin Camp, Inc.*
14,15: Ginger Chih from Peter Arnold*; Clyde H. Smith from Peter Arnold*; Robert Buchbinder*; Mary Eleanor Browning, DPI*; Serge Seymour from Barbara Grinnell*
16,17: Ozzie Sweet*; Allied Mills, Inc.*; *Childcraft* photo; Phoebe Dunn, DPI*
18,19: Jackie Geyer
20–25: Kinuko Craft
26,27: *Childcraft* photos
28,29: Malcolm S. Kirk from Peter Arnold*; Paula Wright, Animals Animals*; *Childcraft* photos
30–59: Joe Cellini; Jean Helmer
60,61: Jackie Geyer
62–71: Darrell Wiskur
72,73: Mike Mariano
74,75: Mike Mariano; Thomas Nebbia, DPI*
76,77: David McCall Johnston
78,79: David McCall Johnston; Oriental Institute, University of Chicago*
80,81: Christian Mundt, Tom Stack & Assoc.*; C. J. Carley, U.S. Fish & Wildlife Service*; Warren Garst, Tom Stack & Assoc.*; Jettie Griffin*
82,83: Michael Hampshire; *Childcraft* photo
84,85: Michael Hampshire; Jettie Griffin*
86–91: Michael Hampshire; *Childcraft* photos
92,93: Jackie Geyer
94–103: Allen Daniel
104,105: Michael Hampshire; Ken-L Ration photo*
106,107: Ruth Sanderson
108,109: J. Pugh, DeWys, Inc.*
110–113: Ken-L Ration photo*; Leslie Morrill
114–115: Ken-L Ration photo*; Michael Hampshire
116,117: Wide World*; Mike Mariano
118–125: *Childcraft* photo; Mike Mariano
126,127: Ken-L Ration photo*; Ruth Sanderson
128,129: Jackie Geyer
130–139: Robert Byrd

140,141: *Wilderness Champion,* J. B. Lippincott Company; *Sounder,* Harper & Row, Publishers, Inc.; *The Hundred and One Dalmatians,* The Viking Press; *Lassie Come Home,* Holt, Rinehart and Winston*; From *Call of the Wild* by Jack London. Special contents copyright © 1965 by Grosset & Dunlap, Inc. Used by permission of publisher* (*Childcraft* photo)
142,143: Anubis from the tomb of Tutankhamen, Egyptian Museum, Cairo (F. L. Kenett, © Rainbird Publishing Group, Ltd.)*; Prehistoric painting located at Sefar on the Tassili N'Ajjer Plateau, Algeria (Douglas Mazonowicz Gallery of Prehistoric Paintings, New York City)*
144,145: Museum of Archeology, Florence, Italy (SCALA)*; Museo Civico, Oderzo, Italy (SCALA)*; Pompei, Italy (SCALA)*
146,147: Illuminated manuscript of Antoine Macault presenting to Francis I his translation of Diodore of Sicily, Conde Museum, Chantilly, France (Giraudon)*; Pottery dog from Colima, Museum of Anthropology, Mexico City (Robert Frerck)*; "Madame Charpentier and Her Children" by Renoir, The Metropolitan Museum of Art, New York City, Wolfe Fund, 1907*
148,149: Bettmann Archive; Australian Information Service*
150,151: Warrensburg Chamber of Commerce*; Robert H. Glaze, Artstreet*; Orion Press from Photri*
152,153: Jerry Pinkney
154,155: Rare Coin Company of America, Inc. (*Childcraft* photo); Ray Johnsen (*Childcraft* photos); stamps, *Childcraft* photos
156,157: © 1976 by United Feature Syndicate*; *Rivets* by George Sixta, Field Newspaper Syndicate*; © Walt Disney Productions
158,159: Jackie Geyer
160–169: Joe Isom
170,171: Robert H. Glaze, Artstreet*; The Seeing Eye, Inc. (*Childcraft* photos)
172,173: The Seeing Eye, Inc. (*Childcraft* photos)
174,175: Photri*
176,177: Chicago Police Dept. (*Childcraft* photos)
178,179: U.S. Customs Service (*Childcraft* photo)
180,181: *Childcraft* photo
182,183: Paul J. Quirico*; Australian Information Service*
184,185: Ringling Bros. and Barnum & Bailey Combined Shows, Inc. (*Childcraft* photos)
186,187: Courtesy of Mulberry Square Productions*; Radnitz/Mattel Productions, Inc.*; *Childcraft* photos by John Hamilton, Globe
188,189: Ken-L Ration photo
190–193: *Childcraft* photos
194,195: Ed Dubrowsky, Taurus*; Mildred F. Mitchell*
196,197: Everett C. Johnson, DeWys, Inc.*
198,199: Thomas Zimmermann, FPG*
200,201: Jackie Geyer
202–213: Jerry Pinkney
214,215: George Suyeoka
216,217: Mike Mariano
218,219: Kinuko Craft
220–225: Joe Veno
226,227: Pat Bargielski
228,229: David McCall Johnston
230–233: Michael Eagle
234,235: Jackie Geyer
236–245: Kinuko Craft
246,247: Virginia Kay*
248–252: *Childcraft* photos
254,255: *Childcraft* photos; Marge Moran
256–259: *Childcraft* photos
260,261: Jerry Pinkney
262–267: *Childcraft* photos
268,269: Doris Pinney, Camera Clix*
270,271: *Childcraft* photo by Alan Beck
272,273: Jackie Geyer
274–292: Robert Keys

Index

This index is an alphabetical list of the important things covered in both words and pictures in this book. The index shows you what page or pages each thing is on. For example, if you want to find out what the book tells about a particular breed of dog, such as the Collie, look under **Collie.** You will find a group of words, called an entry, like this: **Collie** (dog), 280, *with picture.* This entry tells you that you can read about the Collie on page 280. The words *with picture* tell you that there is a picture of the Collie on this page, too. Sometimes, the book only tells you about a thing and does not show a picture. Then the words *with picture* will not be in the entry. It will look like this: **doghouse,** 257. Sometimes, there is *only* a picture of a thing in the book. Then the word *picture* will appear before the page number, like this: **Dingo** (dog), *picture,* 75.